I0430200

ENERGY NEEDS IN ASIA: THE U.S. LIQUEFIED NATURAL GAS OPTION

HEARING

BEFORE THE

SUBCOMMITTEE ON ASIA AND THE PACIFIC

OF THE

COMMITTEE ON FOREIGN AFFAIRS
HOUSE OF REPRESENTATIVES

ONE HUNDRED THIRTEENTH CONGRESS

SECOND SESSION

_____

MAY 29, 2014

_____

Serial No. 113–171

_____

Printed for the use of the Committee on Foreign Affairs

Available via the World Wide Web: http://www.foreignaffairs.house.gov/ or
http://www.gpo.gov/fdsys/

_____

U.S. GOVERNMENT PRINTING OFFICE

88–106PDF   WASHINGTON : 2014

_____

For sale by the Superintendent of Documents, U.S. Government Printing Office
Internet: bookstore.gpo.gov   Phone: toll free (866) 512–1800; DC area (202) 512–1800
Fax: (202) 512–2104   Mail: Stop IDCC, Washington, DC 20402–0001

COMMITTEE ON FOREIGN AFFAIRS

EDWARD R. ROYCE, California, *Chairman*

CHRISTOPHER H. SMITH, New Jersey
ILEANA ROS-LEHTINEN, Florida
DANA ROHRABACHER, California
STEVE CHABOT, Ohio
JOE WILSON, South Carolina
MICHAEL T. McCAUL, Texas
TED POE, Texas
MATT SALMON, Arizona
TOM MARINO, Pennsylvania
JEFF DUNCAN, South Carolina
ADAM KINZINGER, Illinois
MO BROOKS, Alabama
TOM COTTON, Arkansas
PAUL COOK, California
GEORGE HOLDING, North Carolina
RANDY K. WEBER SR., Texas
SCOTT PERRY, Pennsylvania
STEVE STOCKMAN, Texas
RON DeSANTIS, Florida
DOUG COLLINS, Georgia
MARK MEADOWS, North Carolina
TED S. YOHO, Florida
SEAN DUFFY, Wisconsin

ELIOT L. ENGEL, New York
ENI F.H. FALEOMAVAEGA, American
  Samoa
BRAD SHERMAN, California
GREGORY W. MEEKS, New York
ALBIO SIRES, New Jersey
GERALD E. CONNOLLY, Virginia
THEODORE E. DEUTCH, Florida
BRIAN HIGGINS, New York
KAREN BASS, California
WILLIAM KEATING, Massachusetts
DAVID CICILLINE, Rhode Island
ALAN GRAYSON, Florida
JUAN VARGAS, California
BRADLEY S. SCHNEIDER, Illinois
JOSEPH P. KENNEDY III, Massachusetts
AMI BERA, California
ALAN S. LOWENTHAL, California
GRACE MENG, New York
LOIS FRANKEL, Florida
TULSI GABBARD, Hawaii
JOAQUIN CASTRO, Texas

AMY PORTER, *Chief of Staff*   THOMAS SHEEHY, *Staff Director*
JASON STEINBAUM, *Democratic Staff Director*

SUBCOMMITTEE ON ASIA AND THE PACIFIC

STEVE CHABOT, Ohio, *Chairman*

DANA ROHRABACHER, California
MATT SALMON, Arizona
MO BROOKS, Alabama
GEORGE HOLDING, North Carolina
SCOTT PERRY, Pennsylvania
DOUG COLLINS, Georgia

ENI F.H. FALEOMAVAEGA, American
  Samoa
AMI BERA, California
TULSI GABBARD, Hawaii
BRAD SHERMAN, California
GERALD E. CONNOLLY, Virginia
WILLIAM KEATING, Massachusetts

CONTENTS

Page

WITNESSES

Mr. Mikkal E. Herberg, Research Director, Energy Security Program, The National Bureau of Asian Research 7
Ms. Jane Nakano, Fellow, Energy and National Security Program, Center for Strategic and International Studies 14
Ms. Diane Leopold, President, Dominion Energy, Dominion 23

LETTERS, STATEMENTS, ETC., SUBMITTED FOR THE HEARING

Mr. Mikkal E. Herberg: Prepared statement 9
Ms. Jane Nakano: Prepared statement 16
Ms. Diane Leopold: Prepared statement 25

APPENDIX

Hearing notice...48
Hearing minutes..49
The Honorable Gerald E. Connolly, a Representative in Congress from the Commonwealth of Virginia: Prepared statement 50

ENERGY NEEDS IN ASIA: THE U.S. LIQUEFIED NATURAL GAS OPTION

THURSDAY, MAY 29, 2014

House of Representatives,
Subcommittee on Asia and the Pacific,
Committee on Foreign Affairs,
Washington, DC.

The committee met, pursuant to notice, at 2 o'clock p.m., in room 2172 Rayburn House Office Building, Hon. Steve Chabot (chairman of the subcommittee) presiding.

Mr. CHABOT. Good afternoon, and welcome to this afternoon's subcommittee hearing. I want to thank the gentleman from California, Mr. Bera, for serving as today's ranking member and also thank our distinguished panel of witnesses here this afternoon for joining us. We will get to them in just a minute.

This hearing was called to examine the growing need for liquefied natural gas, LNG, in Asia and the United States' role in supplying this energy resource to the region. As Asia's economy continues to rapidly grow, and its population increases, it will unquestionably drive the demand for energy ever higher. Countries in the region are looking for accessible, reliable, and cheap energy, and because of the natural gas boom here in America, the U.S. is evolving into an ideal choice to supply countries thirsty for this resource.

If the U.S. chooses to become a net exporter of LNG and it can manage to reach agreements with major consumers, it will not only strengthen our strategic alliances but it will also aid in the recovery of the U.S. economy.

According to the International Energy Association, global energy demand will increase by 43 percent by 2035 and much of this rising demand will be due to the growing Asian economies. China alone is expected to consume two times the amount of energy as the United States and will account for around 25 percent of the total world energy demand. In Japan, the Fukushima disaster resulted in a near total shutdown of its nuclear reactors and as a result, it is now paying some of the highest prices in the world for LNG— almost $15 per unit last month—to make up for its energy shortfall.

Due to these rising costs, Japan and India, in particular, are reviewing potential suppliers of LNG in an effort to obtain gas that is less expensive than that provided by current suppliers such as Malaysian, Indonesian, Australian and Qatari gas, which is linked to the price of oil—U.S. gas is not. It would seem to me that supplying gas that is not determined by the price of oil would be considerably beneficial for the Asian market, as well as for U.S. suppliers. To do this, I believe it is critical that the administration increase the pace at which it is working to make U.S. LNG supplies more accessible to countries such as India and Japan, so that U.S. supplies can satisfy Asia's increasing demand.

Here in the U.S., we are producing over 70 billion cubic feet of natural gas per day and by 2017 we may produce more natural gas than we consume. Net energy imports are expected to fall to as low as 4 percent by 2040 and according to some experts, we could be completely energy self-sufficient even sooner.

Just a few years ago, the U.S. required LNG import terminals to relieve our demand for gas; those terminals will now function as LNG export terminals as they undergo conversions and companies build their liquefication capabilities. We currently have a temporary export capacity of 7 billion cubic feet per day but we have the capacity to export up to 38 billion cubic feet per day if all applications for LNG export are approved. And not surprisingly, U.S. producers are lining up to supply the global market with this abundant stock of LNG where, a large portion of these natural gas supplies will be sold to countries throughout Asia.

The increase in unconventional energy production has already resulted in significant benefits for the U.S. economy. Perhaps one of the greatest impacts of this new energy abundance is the effect that it has had on domestic employment. In 2012, over 2 million jobs were either directly or indirectly the result of unconventional energy production. It also has decreased the trade deficit by more than $164 billion over the last 5 years. Manufacturing has been revitalized. Many small towns in rural regions have experienced a surge in economic growth. Moreover, the thriving natural gas industry has afforded the U.S. a strong competitive global advantage. We should encourage an American competitive edge—particularly in light of ongoing conflicts in the Middle East and Russia's recent behavior.

Supporting LNG exports to Asia—the region with the greatest future energy demand—should be a crucial component of this administration's strategic rebalance toward Asia. Ensuring our allies' and partners' energy security will demonstrate the U.S.' commitment to the region. Many of my colleagues and I have insisted that the administration support the rebalance with tangible actions as opposed to thinly defined proclamations. Promoting LNG exports is a perfect way to do so.

U.S. LNG also offers a safe and reliable option to countries in Asia which may otherwise purchase gas from states that often neglect the rule of law, such as Russia and Iran. In fact, just last week, China signed a $400 billion deal to import natural gas from Russia for the next 30 years. This follows Russia's announcement that it plans to increase its presence in the Asia-Pacific markets to broaden its exports and attract investment.

Now is the time for the United States to seriously consider undertaking a more significant role in Asia's energy markets. A strong and engaged U.S. economic presence in Asia will ensure that our regional allies have a reliable access to the energy supply they need and will help to support our strategic interests.

I think we all look forward to hearing from our distinguished witnesses this afternoon and I would now like to yield to Mr. Bera for 5 minutes to make an opening statement.

Mr. BERA. Thank you, Chairman Chabot, and thank you to the witnesses for being here. This is an incredibly important conversation for us to have as we start to review our current positions but then also look at future policies on U.S. energy security and LNG exports.

We know that demand for LNG exports certainly is steadily rising partly in—because of the necessity of coming up with more environmentally friendly fuel sources and we know LNG produces less emissions and pollutants as compared to the oil and coal industries.

I also recognize as we debate and look at our policy for LNG exports that there is an opportunity by increasing exports to strengthen and stabilize our U.S. allies, and that is an important component of this discussion at the same time while reducing our nation's trade deficits.

In addition, as we look at liquid natural gas and look at natural gas in general we also have to be mindful of the domestic opportunities that we have here in keeping our energy prices at a very competitive level, particularly as we set policies and revive a manufacturing sector here at home. You know, this energy renaissance does give us a real opportunity here to revive manufacturing and make us more globally competitive.

So that is certainly another component in this. When we think about what LNG exports can do, you know, I am going to use an example of one of my colleagues, a close friend, Dr. Charles Boustany, who represents the Third District in Louisiana, and here is what it means to his district.

Sempra is one of the three largest LNG export facilities in Louisiana and it was recently permitted by the Department of Energy to export to non-FTA countries. The estimates there are that they will add 130 high-paying direct jobs while retaining 60 existing jobs.

In addition, Sempra will be able to create an additional 610 new permanent jobs along with 3,000 construction jobs during peak activity. That is not a small amount and certainly is an important component of this.

That said, as I mentioned before, we have to understand some of the concerns as we increase LNG exports of the possible ramifications on gas prices here domestically in the United States and that does have to be a component of this as well as the environmental impact that additional LNG production will have.

As a nation, we have got to be responsible and prudent when it comes to health and safety standards as well in regards to energy production. I do believe that we need to move toward a clean energy future that will protect the health of the our families and protect our planet.

The increased use of natural gas both in the U.S. and abroad is one of those components that can help us address our future environmental concerns and help reduce carbon emissions that contribute to global warming.

In addition, increased use of natural gas will reduce the levels of other pollutants and, you know, certainly, will help us reduce our reliance on coal and can help us with some of our ally countries.

The path to clean energy will require a skilled labor force that works together to power a cleaner, more efficient society and, you know, again, as we debate LNG exports and look at this from multiple different facets let us certainly keep climate change in mind, other pollutants in mind.

At the same time, let us make sure we are doing things strategically both to create domestic jobs and domestic employments both in the export phase but then also keep manufacturing in mind.

So I look forward to the testimony of our witnesses and, certainly, I yield back.

Mr. CHABOT. Thank you. The gentleman yields back.

The gentleman from Pennsylvania, Mr. Perry, is recognized for 1 minute to make an opening statement.

Mr. PERRY. Thank you, Mr. Chairman. Thank you to the testifiers for being here. Over the past 3 years, just seven of the applications to export natural gas to non-free trade agreement countries have received Department of Energy approval while 23 are still pending.

If all the approved non-FTA projects were constructed and operating, the United States would be second only behind Qatar with the most LNG export capacity. Increased natural gas exports could also put into action the Obama administration's stated foreign policy goal of a pivot to Asia.

As in Europe, U.S. LNG exports have the potential to weaken the market power of incumbent LNG providers to Asia such as Russia by increasing the negotiating power of consumers while providing a supply that is free from politically-based disruptions.

Also, increased U.S. exports could provide partners in Asia and elsewhere a stable supply in the event of further violence in the Middle East.

With that, I look forward to hearing the testimony and I yield back.

Mr. CHABOT. The gentleman yields back. The gentleman from California, Mr. Sherman, who is the ranking member of the Terrorism, Nonproliferation, and Trade Subcommittee, is recognized for 1 minute to make an opening statement.

Mr. SHERMAN. Mr. Chairman, I enjoyed our trip to Asia and there is one thing I learned from Randy Weber and that is there are five ports in the 14th Congressional District of Texas and according to Randy every one of them ought to have an LNG export facility.

If we were to grant all the licenses that Randy would propose, we would raise production of natural gas in the United States. We would raise the price of the natural gas in the United States.

Our manufacturers would lose the competitive advantage they have over Asian manufacturers since they are paying about a third for the natural gas that the Asian manufacturers are.

I mean, the Asian manufacturers, if we exported to Asia, would see a lower cost of natural gas and would become even more ferocious competitors.

From an environmental standpoint, if increased natural gas production displaces coal that is good for global warming. I have got a lot of environmentalists who think it will simply displace conservation, that somehow everyone will live like my friend Ed Begley if only—if only we can stop every energy production and all energy exports.

Finally, I believe in the full committee there was considerable discussion of how exporting natural gas to the Ukraine would be a way to deal with Russia, and I pointed out then and I should point out here the Japanese and others in Asia will pay at least 50 percent more for that natural gas than the Ukrainians are used to paying the Russians for the natural gas.

So not—so far I have seen no proposals to increase our U.S. taxes so that we can subsidize Ukrainian purchases of American natural gas. That being the case, I think that if we are going to be exporting natural gas it will be within the jurisdiction of this subcommittee, and I yield back to its chairman.

Mr. CHABOT. Thank you very much. The gentleman yields back.

The gentleman from California, Mr. Rohrabacher, who is the chairman of the Europe, Eurasia, and Emerging Threats Subcommittee, is recognized for a minute to make an opening statement.

Mr. ROHRABACHER. Thank you very much, Mr. Chairman. Let us just get this straight. Providing natural gas, whether it is through LNG or any other way, to people who want to buy it and need it is not a hostile act toward Russia.

Unfortunately, too many people are basically describing this within that framework. Increasing the level of energy in the world and increasing the productivity and the actual—facilitating the distribution of natural gas or any other energy source is not hostile toward any one country and in fact it is increasing the wealth level of all people.

That is why I would suggest that we should be supporting every effort to increase whether it is liquefied natural gas or sales to various countries but we should also be supporting the various pipeline proposals that we see in various parts of Asia today and we should be, of course, supporting the development of our own natural gas resources in the United States.

These are all positive things so let us not get too caught up in the strategic chess game to know that what we are really talking about is people having more energy to live better lives, whoever they are.

Thank you very much, Mr. Chairman.

Mr. CHABOT. Thank you. The gentleman yields back.

The gentleman from North Carolina, Mr. Holding, is recognized for 1 minute.

Mr. HOLDING. Thank you, Mr. Chairman. As energy demands rapidly increase in the Asia-Pacific region because of growing population and manufacturing needs, Asian nations are looking for any opportunity to import new supplies.

Mr. Chairman, Asia is energy hungry. With the new technologies unlocking once unrecoverable resources in our nation, America is energy rich.

With all the talk about our rebalance to Asia, we hear a lot from the administration about increasing our diplomatic presence and strengthening our mil-to-mil cooperation with our Asian partners.

Increasing our energy ties specifically through export of LNG should be at the forefront of the rebalance discussion given the geopolitical implications. I look forward to this hearing.

I look forward to hearing from our witnesses today about the unique position we are in right now to expand our LNG exports to Asia.

Thank you, Mr. Chairman. I yield back.

Mr. CHABOT. Thank you, and the Chair thanks all the members for their opening statements. I thought every one of them was quite good and I will now introduce the panel here this afternoon.

We will begin with Mikkal E. Herberg, who is the research director of National Bureau of Asian Research's Energy Security Program. He is also a senior lecturer at the Graduate School of International Relations and Pacific Studies, University of California, San Diego. Previously, Mr. Herberg spent 20 years in the oil industry in strategic planning roles for ARCO where he was director for global energy and economics. He also headed country risk analysis and was responsible for advising executive management on risk conditions and investment strategies in regions where ARCO had major investments. Prior to that, he worked as the director of portfolio risk management and director for emerging markets at ARCO. Mr. Herberg writes and speaks extensively on Asian energy issues, the energy industry, governments and major research institutions globally and we welcome you here this afternoon.

I would next like to introduce Jane Nakano, who is a fellow in the Energy and National Security Program at the Center for Strategic and International Studies. Her areas of research include energy security issues in Asia, global nuclear energy trends and global natural gas market dynamics. Prior to joining CSIS, she was with the Department of Energy and served as the lead staff on U.S. energy engagements with China and Japan. She was responsible for coordinating Department of Energy engagement in Asia and she has worked extensively with China, Japan, Indonesia, North Korea and the Asia Pacific Economic Cooperation.

Previously, she served at the U.S. Embassy in Tokyo as special assistant to the energy attaché. Ms. Nakano holds a bachelor's degree from Georgetown University School of Foreign Service and a master's degree from Columbia University School of International and Public Affairs. We welcome you here this afternoon.

Finally, we have Diane Leopold, who served as president of Dominion Energy since January of this year. Previously, she held management roles in several business units. Most recently, she worked as senior vice president of Business Development and Generation Construction and senior vice president of Dominion Transmission. Prior to her work with Dominion, she has held several engineering positions at Potomac Electric Power Company. Ms. Leopold sits as a vice president of the board of trustees of the Virginia Commonwealth University Foundation and is also a member of the board of directors of the Interstate Natural Gas Association of America. She received her bachelor's degree in mechanical and electrical engineering from the University of Sussex and a master's degree in electrical engineering from George Washington University. She also holds an MBA from Virginia Commonwealth University and we welcome you here this afternoon, Ms. Leopold.

I am sure that the witnesses are probably familiar with our 5-minute rule. Each of you will have 5 minutes to testify. A yellow light should come on when you have about a minute to wrap up, then the red light comes on. If you could wrap up as quickly as possible, we would greatly appreciate it.

Mr. Herberg, you are recognized for 5 minutes.

STATEMENT OF MR. MIKKAL E. HERBERG, RESEARCH DIREC-TOR, ENERGY SECURITY PROGRAM, THE NATIONAL BUREAU OF ASIAN RESEARCH

Mr. HERBERG. Thank you, Chairman Chabot, Ranking Member Bera, distinguished members of the subcommittee. Thank you for inviting me to share my views on prospects for U.S. LNG supplies to Asia.

It is hard to overstate how important LNG is to the energy and economic outlook in Asia. Asia is two-thirds of the global LNG market. Japan alone is more than one-third of the global LNG market.

LNG meets 100 percent of Japan's natural gas needs as well as South Korea, Taiwan, key allies in the region. So LNG looms very large in Asia's economic future so I think the U.S. opportunity to supply large amounts of LNG is, you know, the proverbial win-win-win.

It helps allies, provides more supplies, reduces the potential for single suppliers or few suppliers to dominate the marketplace and in a lot of ways it is—you know, it is clean energy. Places like China and India so dependent on coal, we need to do everything we can to encourage more natural gas use in Asia.

So I think this is one of those really positive opportunities we have. Lots of supplies heading toward Asia from a variety of places. Australia is gearing up to become the largest LNG exporter very soon by the end of the decade.

Russia—probably two big projects will come online in Russia in the next 10 years, although that is subject to a lot of Kremlin politics, East Africa offshore and, of course, the U.S. supplies.

U.S. supplies are already benefiting Asia. There were huge projects coming online from Qatar in 2009, 2010 and 2011 that were destined for the U.S. market, which we thought was going to be a large LNG importer.

Well, that gas not coming here was available to meet Japan's increased needs in the wake of the Fukushima crisis. Otherwise, Japan's problem and Asia's LNG problem would have been much, much worse than it turned out to be. So we are already—we are already benefiting the region.

This issue of the supply in the U.S. domestic market, at $4.50 gas prices here and transported to Asia we are talking about $10 or $11 LNG supplies from the U.S. into Asia. That looks good when $15 is the current LNG price.

But all you have to do is raise U.S. domestic gas prices by a little bit and reduce Asian LNG prices by a little bit and at $12 or $13 it becomes a wash. So in a sense the market—shipping to Asia will be limited in effect by the marketplace at—probably at a relatively modest U.S. domestic natural gas price. I think that is an important element to keep in the discussion.

The key beneficiaries, clearly, will be Japan, South Korea. Japan has contracts already for 17 million tons of U.S. LNG in the current projects. They are partners in four of the largest projects.

They are desperately looking forward to increased supplies from the U.S. both as an incremental supply, as a diversification to a secure supply source as well as the introduction of Henry Hub market flexible pricing into this very rigid oil-linked pricing system for LNG in Asia. That is what gets you $15, $16, $17 LNG prices today.

So the introduction of the new pricing mechanism is critical to the Asian LNG consumers, particularly Japan and South Korea. So I think it is important that both of them will benefit tremendously from the additional supply and, obviously, these are key strategic partners in Asia and I think that is a very direct benefit and strengthen our ties.

It is not an accident that LNG exports to Japan were mentioned in the most recent visit of President Obama to Japan. It is critical on their list. I think the best way to bolster the impact of our LNG exports is largely let the market works maximize the amount of LNG going to Asia and maximize the development of shale gas development here in the U.S.

Of course, with the proper regulatory safeguards I think that is critically important. It means lower prices, diversified supplies and other benefits for the region.

And it is probably going to be a very important potential benefit relationships both with India and China. China is going to be a huge LNG importer in the future and some of this gas—LNG will make its way to China.

One final point—more gas, more LNG to Asia—the gas—the LNG market is not a global market. It is a highly regionalised market. But as our gas goes to Asia in significant supplies, that is going to at the margin displace swing producer LNG from places like Qatar and West African LNG producers and that gas is going to eventually make its way to Europe.

So indirectly that gas can feed into a more diversified LNG and gas supply in Europe and we all know those issues related to Europe's heavy dependence on Russia. It is not one to one. Europe has to get their pipeline system straightened out because you cannot wheel gas around the region effectively given the pipeline constraints and national monopolies.

That is important for Europe to get straightened up. But our supplies will displace and shift supplies toward Europe and I think that is critically important. So I will stop with that.

I think we have got a lot of benefits that can come from this. With the proper regulation of the shale gas development we have an opportunity to really be an important source of gas and energy security to Asia.

Thank you.

[The prepared statement of Mr. Herberg follows:]

Mikkal E. Herberg
Research Director, Energy Security Program
The National Bureau of Asian Research
Testimony to the Subcommittee on Asia and the Pacific
U.S. House Committee on Foreign Affairs
May 29, 2014

Mr. Chairman, Ranking Member Bera, and distinguished Subcommittee members:

Thank you for inviting me here to share my views on U.S. policy toward supplying liquefied natural gas (LNG) resources to Asia. My name is Mikkal Herberg and I am Research Director for the Energy Security Program at The National Bureau of Asian Research (NBR). These views are mine alone and do not reflect the views of NBR which does not take institutional positions on any policy issue.

The Energy Security Program at NBR has been studying these issues and last June 2013, held a day-long workshop in Washington, D.C. on "Asia's Uncertain LNG Future" and issued a report in November 2013. It concluded that LNG will play an increasingly important role in ensuring Asia's future energy security as well as helping shift Asia's coal-intensive energy fuel mix towards a more environmentally sustainable path. Asia traditionally accounts for two-thirds of global LNG consumption. Japan and South Korea have alone have been the large, base-load buyers of LNG, typically accounting for one-half of global LNG consumption. Asia's LNG consumption is expected to grow dramatically over the next two decades as China and India boost their LNG imports and as Japan and South Korea substitute LNG for declining nuclear energy supplies. Even Southeast Asia, traditionally a significant exporter of LNG to Northeast Asia, is seeing a dramatic shift in consumption and will become increasingly dependent of imported LNG.

This positive outlook, however, is also somewhat uncertain. The outlook for LNG demand growth in China, Japan, South Korea, and India is uncertain as each grapples with domestic energy supply challenges and critical policy decisions over the role of nuclear energy, environmental goals, and gas pricing challenges. On the supply side, while it is clear that substantial new supplies will be coming to Asia from Australia, Russia, the U.S. (including Alaska), Canada, and offshore East Africa, there are enormous questions over the rising cost of LNG projects, Russia's gas and LNG decisions about investing in its far eastern gas supplies and infrastructure, and domestic policy constraints in the U.S. and Canada. Finally, the evolution of LNG prices in Asia is critical to the scale and pace of Asia's LNG demand growth. High oil-linked prices that prevail in Asia today threaten to slow the growth in use of LNG. In this regard, U.S. pricing of LNG potentially linked to market-driven domestic Henry-Hub gas prices could be an important factor in strengthening and re-shaping Asia's LNG future.

Both in LNG supply and in pricing terms, potential U.S. LNG exports to Asia have the potential to play a very important and positive role in Asia's energy and energy security future. In fact, the boom in U.S. shale gas production is already benefiting Asia and especially Japan. Seven years ago it was expected that the U.S. would be a very large importer of LNG by 2014, competing with Japan and other importers for global LNG supplies. Instead, the U.S., combined with Canadian gas imports, is now essentially self-sufficient in natural gas on a North American basis. As a result, large new LNG supplies from Qatar that came on line in 2010-2011 that were originally destined for the U.S. market suddenly became available to help meet Japan's increased LNG needs in the wake of the Fukushima nuclear disaster and shutdown of Japan's nuclear generation capacity. Japan's nuclear energy crisis would have been far more damaging to Japan's economy and energy security without those unexpected LNG supplies freed up by U.S. shale gas production. South Korea has benefited similarly.

Questions about U.S. LNG exports to Asia and the potential economic and strategic implications require some discussion of potential volumes of U.S. LNG exports and assumptions about U.S. natural gas and Asian LNG prices. Forecasts from Japan's Institute of Energy Economics (IEEJ) suggest that Asia's LNG demand will roughly double between 2013 and 2040, from 180 million metric tonnes per year (mmt/y) to 360 mmt/y in 2040. As of early 2014 the U.S. Department of Energy has issued permits for five potential U.S. LNG export projects for over 9 billion cubic feet per day (bcf/d), equivalent to roughly 65-70 mmt/y of LNG that could come on line between 2015 and 2025. Many more projects are in line for approvals for a total potential of more than 100 mmt/y. Hence, technically U.S. LNG could be a major source of Asia's rising LNG needs.

However, how much of that LNG actually gets developed will depend heavily on the cost and price of that LNG and the evolution of LNG prices in Asia and globally. Asia's current oil-linked spot market price for LNG is roughly $16-17 per million btu's (mmbtu), well above Europe's average $9-11 gas prices and U.S. Henry Hub prices presently around $4.50. With a liquefaction and transportation cost estimate of roughly $6.00 per mmbtu to send U.S. Gulf coast LNG to Asia, U.S. gas *at current prices* would be highly competitive in Asia's market. Asia would also benefit from the introduction of flexible, market-based U.S. gas prices into regional LNG pricing formulas.

Nevertheless, the share of U.S. LNG in Asia's future market depends ultimately on the evolution of U.S. gas prices as well as the evolution of Asia's LNG prices. Many expect U.S. natural gas prices to gradually rise in the future as domestic demand grows strongly. In other words, hub-based pricing is no long-term guarantee of low prices. At the same time, many forecasts also suggest that Asian LNG prices should decline over the next decade towards $12-13 per mmbtu as large new supplies hit the market from Australia, Russia, the U.S. and Canada, as well as offshore East Africa. While all this is highly speculative, the point is that the future volume of U.S. LNG exports to Asia will ultimately depend on Asian LNG demand and prices and

U.S. natural gas prices, rather than how much LNG supply is permitted by the U.S. government. At $6.00 U.S. gas prices and $12-13 Asian LNG prices the two markets largely equilibrate and the commercial incentive to invest in new U.S. LNG supplies for the Asian market disappear. The implication is that U.S. exports could be 30 mmt/y by 2025 or could be 80 mmt/y depending on these market developments.

It is within these broad boundaries of LNG market dynamics and prospects that I address the Subcommittee's questions.

It seems clear that the largest buyers of U.S. LNG are likely to be Japan and South Korea. Both have substantial needs to contract for new long-term LNG supplies as many of their existing long-term LNG contracts gradually expire over the next 10 years and as each faces similar constraints on their nuclear power capacities. Wood Mackenzie consultants estimate that together their incremental un-contracted LNG volumes will rise to 30 mmt/y by 2020. Japan is most focused on securing future U.S. LNG supplies for many reasons, mostly related to the Fukushima nuclear crisis and the very high cost of their LNG supplies at high oil-linked prices. According to the IEEJ, Japan's trading houses and large utilities currently have offtake agreements to buy 17 mmt/y of LNG from planned U.S. LNG projects. These Japanese companies have equity ownership stakes in four major U.S. LNG projects. Japanese companies are also participating in four proposed Canadian LNG projects. South Korea also will be a significant buyer of U.S. LNG. South Korea is also facing its own nuclear energy crisis due to the shutdown of three of its 23 nuclear generating plants due to a corruption scandal over fraudulent parts and substandard maintainance. State-owned KOGAS has a contract to buy 3.5 mmt/y with the Sabine Pass project.

Substantial U.S. LNG exports to Japan and South Korea can have important knock-on effects in strengthening our respective strategic alliances with our strongest security partners in Asia. For Japan, energy security is national security. The Fukushima crisis represents the most serious energy crisis faced by Japan since the 1970s. The notion that the U.S. would not export LNG to Japan due to the lack of a Free Trade Agreement when it simultaneously would export to South Korea, which has a Free Trade Agreement with the U.S., would cause real damage to the most important U.S. strategic alliance in Asia. Both Japan and South Korea have been disappointed in the lack of progress with Moscow in developing more LNG supplies from Far East Russia for Northeast Asia as a result of lack of investment from Moscow. For South Korea the availability of new LNG supplies from the U.S. helps them diversify their 100% import dependence on LNG. South Korea has few other options for natural gas. Efforts over the past decade to forge an agreement to build a natural gas pipeline to bring Russian gas supplies across North Korea to South Korea have been stymied by North Korean intransigence or Russian disinterest. For both Japan and South Korea, the opportunity to incorporate market-based U.S. gas pricing into their LNG contracts has the potential to substantially reduce their LNG import costs. No other LNG supply source promises to introduce a new, potentially more favorable pricing mechanism.

The best way for the U.S. to bolster its influence in Asia in terms of its LNG is to maximize the amount of U.S. LNG available for Asia, as well as Europe, albeit within the framework of allowing markets to ultimately determine the volumes and prices. I would not advocate trying to use LNG exports or availability as some sort of diplomatic tool. U.S. influence will come from being a substantial, reliable, and price competitive source of LNG to the global market. Lower LNG prices in Asia and more reliable supplies strengthen our role in the region where secure LNG supplies are a critical dimension of economic prosperity in Asia and, therefore, for the U.S.

Substantial U.S. LNG exports to the global LNG market will also reduce the potential diplomatic leverage of other LNG suppliers who may be intent on using energy supplies for diplomatic leverage. For example, although most U.S. LNG exports will go to Asia where current LNG prices are much higher, more LNG for Asia means that other LNG supplies will be available to Europe which can, in the very long run, potentially reduce Europe's reliance on Russian pipeline gas. Gas trade in Europe is complicated and there is no one-to-one relationship between more LNG and reduced Russian gas imports. However, as Europe develops a more integrated gas market with pipeline connections that more fully incorporate the eastern part of Europe that is most dependent on Russian gas into a continental grid, the heavy dependence on Russian gas will be reduced somewhat. This can also help lower LNG and gas prices in Europe. These are some of the reasons Europe is looking to access U.S. LNG supplies as well and a number of European buyers have offtake agreements with U.S. LNG projects.

U.S. LNG supplies to Asia, depending of course on the scale and price, will inevitably compete with supplies from Malaysia, Australia, Qatar, and Russia. There is expected to be a very large expansion in supplies to Asia in the 2015-2023 period as large new supplies begin arriving from Australia, the U.S. Canada, as well as significant new LNG supplies likely from Far East Russian projects. Offshore East Africa seems likely to arrive well after 2020 due to huge infrastructure and investment challenges. Malaysian LNG supplies are not likely to grow between now and 2020 and, as Malaysian domestic natural gas consumption grows strongly in the future, many expect Malaysian LNG exports to gradually decline naturally after 2020. Australia projects appear to be among the most challenged by rising U.S. LNG exports. Australia LNG exports are expected to boom between 2015 and 2020 as nearly 50 mmt/y of new projects come on line, making Australia the world's largest LNG exporter by the early 2020's. However, Australian project costs have skyrocketed due to higher labor, infrastructure, and foreign exchange costs. These supplies will face significant price competition late in the decade as lower cost U.S. LNG supplies to Asia grow. Qatar, currently the largest LNG exporter in the world at 70 mmt/y, is holding its exports stable as the government has in place an LNG development moratorium while it evaluates the production capacity and longevity of its enormous North Dome gas field. Qatar has options that other LNG exporters don't have. Qatar's supplies are very low cost relative to most other LNG exporters. Hence, it can send LNG to Europe or Asia, although clearly Asia is favored today due to higher prices and profitability. However, Qatar can still earn good investment returns on LNG sales in Europe.

China as a potential market for U.S. LNG deserves some attention. China's LNG imports are rising rapidly and it currently imports over 20 mmt/y in 2013. Regasification capacity is being built or planned that could take China to 60-80 mmt/y by the early 2020's. China is seeking to boost natural gas consumption by four-fold between 2010 and 2020 in an effort to reduce the growth in coal use and the damaging air pollution and carbon consequences. How much LNG China might import in the future, though, depends on its pipeline imports and development of domestic gas supplies, including large shale gas resources. The latest Russia-China gas pipeline agreement will provide an additional gas supply starting at the end of the decade. Up to now, China has not shown much interest in U.S. LNG supplies but this seems to be changing. Substantial U.S. LNG exports to China in the future could possibly help reduce tensions between the U.S. and China over energy security issues.

India seems likely to be a relatively modest overall factor in U.S. LNG exports. Due to its geographic location, India's LNG supplies come largely from the Persian Gulf. India imported 15 mmt/y of LNG in 2012, of which 12 mmt/y came from Qatar. However, India is an important trade partner and the U.S. has developed a closer strategic relationship with India over the past decade. India is interested in potentially lower-cost U.S. LNG supplies and its state gas company, GAIL, has a contract to import LNG from the Cove Point LNG project. Lower cost LNG would be important to India since it has struggled with raising domestic natural gas prices to levels that could cover the high cost of imported LNG. Energy and natural gas prices are highly regulated in India and, despite efforts over the past decade to reform prices, maintains energy and gas prices far below what's needed to justify much new investment in energy supplies.

Thank you for your attention and I look forward to answering any questions you might have.

Mr. CHABOT. Thank you very much.

Ms. Nakano, you are recognized for 5 minutes.

STATEMENT OF MS. JANE NAKANO, FELLOW, ENERGY AND NATIONAL SECURITY PROGRAM, CENTER FOR STRATEGIC AND INTERNATIONAL STUDIES

Ms. NAKANO. Good afternoon, Chairman Chabot, Ranking Member Bera and members of the subcommittee. Thank you for the opportunity to testify about the future of liquefied natural gas demand in Asia and the role of U.S. LNG supplies.

It is an honor to appear before the subcommittee and address this very important topic. In the interests of time, I will provide a brief overview of my written testimony and look forward to providing more detail during the question and answer period.

Even before the U.S. LNG shipments to Asia begin later this decade, the ascent of the United States as a major natural gas producer has already demonstrated U.S. strengths to the regional players.

For example, during the supply uncertainty after the Fukushima nuclear crisis, the Persian Gulf gas supplies once destined for the United States prevented a serious supply shortage in Asia.

Also, by delivering a range of macroeconomic benefits, the robust development of shale gas together with tight oil has dampened the United States in decline narrative that emerged after the economic recession of 2008, especially in China. Moreover, the U.S. new energy posture is starting to defuse the geopolitical undertone in Japan's energy relationship with Russia.

The most likely U.S. bilateral relationship to benefit from U.S. LNG supplies is, in my judgment, U.S.-Japan. U.S. LNG supplies would help Japan address its post-Fukushima energy and economic security challenges and the improved economic health of Japan, a key U.S. ally in the region, in turn would further U.S. ability to advance national security objectives in Asia.

Also, in terms of volume, Japan will likely be the largest buyer of U.S. LNG. Japan's large LNG import capacity, the uncertainty over nuclear energy and its robust investment commitment in U.S. shale and U.S. export projects support my judgment. Specifically, about a quarter of the U.S. LNG exports approved to date is expected to go to Japan.

One country in Asia that serves as a significant variable is China, which is forecast to overtake South Korea as the second largest global LNG importer by 2020. However, its domestic shale gas potential, the future volume of pipeline gas import from Central Asia and Russia and the notable absence of Chinese investment commitment in U.S. LNG export projects render it difficult for me to envision China becoming one of the largest importers of U.S. LNG.

As remarkable as the effects of the U.S. shale gas revolution are, there is an inherent danger in extrapolating that LNG resources accord significant geopolitical leverage to the United States.

There is a limit to which privately-held and market allocated resources such as oil and gas could be successfully employed to deliver a specific geopolitical or strategic outcome.

Furthermore, caution is warranted in extrapolating the extent to which U.S. LNG supplies may fundamentally alter the energy relationships between importer countries in Asia and their traditional gas suppliers.

First, by early next decade the Asian LNG market is expected to see new volumes of supplies from new LNG projects in places like Australia and fierce competition may emerge among LNG suppliers. The pace of U.S. LNG export approval greatly influences the degree to which the U.S. LNG supplies can gain a foothold in Asia.

Second, as a series of U.S. export projects come to fruition later this decade, the price differential between U.S. and non-U.S. gas supplies may narrow to the extent that the economic benefit from U.S. LNG may be negligible.

Third, energy export is central to the economic health of many of the traditional supplier countries and many Asian stakeholders believe that the centrality of energy revenue combined with their vast resource levels continue to make them reliable trade partners.

Finally, there are factors exogenous to the U.S. energy posture that are likely to greatly influence the level of LNG exports from Qatar and Malaysia in the future.

A range of factors renders it difficult to forecast the trajectory of future LNG demand outlook for individual countries in Asia or the future composition of LNG suppliers to Asia.

Yet the United States has an important role to play for the greater security of energy supply in Asia and around the world by continuing to espouse principles such as free trade and transparency that are essential for the sound working of the international energy marketplace and the resultant free flow of oil and gas.

The stability that U.S. LNG supplies can induce and/or enhance in Asia is an understated yet significant asset that can underpin the continued U.S. leadership in the region.

Thank you for your time and opportunity to address the subcommittee. I look forward to your questions.

[The prepared statement of Ms. Nakano follows:]

CSIS | CENTER FOR STRATEGIC &
INTERNATIONAL STUDIES

Statement before the House Foreign Affairs Subcommittee
on Asia and the Pacific

"ENERGY NEEDS IN ASIA: THE U.S. LIQUEFIED NATURAL GAS OPTION"

A Statement by

Jane Nakano

Fellow, Energy and National Security Program

Center for Strategic and International Studies (CSIS)

May 29, 2014

2172 Rayburn House Office Building

WWW.CSIS.ORG   1616 RHODE ISLAND AVENUE NW   TEL. (202) 887.0200
WASHINGTON, DC 20036   FAX (202) 775.3199

Good afternoon, Chairman Chabot, Ranking Member Faleomavaega, and members of the Committee. Thank you for the opportunity to testify about the future of liquefied natural gas (LNG) demand in Asia and the role of U.S. LNG supplies. It is an honor to appear before the Subcommittee and address this important topic.

Asia is already the largest LNG importing region in the world, accounting for two thirds of the global trade in LNG today. It is expected that the region will maintain this share for some decades to come. The United States is poised to be an important player in enhancing the security of energy supplies in Asia due to robust U.S. production of shale gas and the LNG export capacity expected to come online in the near future. In the testimony that follows, I will provide some insights as to the nature of the U.S.-Asia LNG trading relationship and what it may portend for bilateral and regional relations.

Question 1: Which Asian countries are expected to be the largest buyers of U.S. LNG and how will these economic ties affect our bilateral relationships?

In my judgment, Japan will be the largest buyer of U.S. LNG. The factors that lead to this judgment are Japan's existing large LNG import capacity, its continued need for cleaner fossil-based fuel in light of nuclear energy uncertainty, and its robust investment commitment in U.S. shale and LNG export projects.

First, with 30 LNG receiving terminals in place, Japan has been the largest importer of LNG in the world for some decades. Japan's geographical feature of being an island country propelled Japan to turn to LNG in the late1960s, when it began importing LNG from Alaska. Five additional LNG terminals are now under construction—anticipated to come online by 2016—to further the country's import capacity (350 bcf/y or 7.19 mmt/y).[1]

Second, the post-Fukushima closure of 54 nuclear power reactors has resulted in surging natural gas demand in Japan to avert a shortfall of 49 gigawatts of electricity supply. Japan's LNG demand increased 24 percent between 2010 and 2012.[2] The country's LNG import volume of 4.3 trillion cubic feet or tcf (or 87 million metric tons or mmt) in 2012 represented 37 percent of the global volume of LNG demand that year and was double the volume imported by the second largest importer of LNG in the world, South Korea.[3] While the Japanese political leadership strives to restart at least some nuclear power plants, the high level of public anxiety over the safety of existing nuclear power plants limits the prospect for a robust return of nuclear power generation in Japan. LNG will thus likely remain a major power source for Japan for some decades to come.

Third, meeting the surge in natural gas demand led Japan to pay $67.7 billion for LNG in 2012, about double the amount spent in 2010. Not surprisingly, Japan ran a large trade deficit of $78 billion that year—170 percent higher than in 2011. Continued nuclear outage and LNG import

---

[1] U.S. Energy Information Administration, 2013. http://www.eia.gov/countries/cab.cfm?fips=ja
[2] Ibid.
[3] Ibid.

reliance further raised Japan's annual trade gap in JFY 2013 to $112 billion—a 40 percent increase year-on-year—and the highest in its history.[4]

The fiscal burden from rising LNG import costs has driven Japan to seek access to competitively priced natural gas supplies around the world, but particularly in the United States, where natural gas prices are deregulated and natural gas is sold through a series of pricing points or hubs, most notably Henry Hub in Louisiana. Current price differentials between the U.S. and Japanese gas markets—about $4-5 per million British thermal unit in the United States and $15–$18 per million British thermal unit in Japan—make U.S. LNG imports commercially viable even after costs are added for liquefaction and shipping. A few major Japanese companies are investing in U.S. shale production projects in places such as the Marcellus shale and the Eagle Ford shale to secure access to cheaper supply at source. Also, Japanese companies have significant investment commitments in U.S. LNG export projects—such as Freeport, Cove Point and Cameron. For example, the total volume of U.S. LNG contracted by the Japanese through 2013—if materialized—would amount to roughly 20 percent (17 mmt/y) of the Japanese imports today.

Also, Japanese companies have had a decades-long LNG trade relationship with Alaska. Although the Alaskan LNG supplies would not likely be shale-based, Japan will most likely be the primary importer of Alaskan LNG once there is a commercial breakthrough in LNG projects there.

The Japanese investment in U.S. shale development and export projects as well as the actual LNG trade would strengthen economic relations between the United States and Japan. Also, LNG supplies would help Japan address its energy security and economic security challenges and the improved economic health of Japan—a key U.S. ally in the region—in turn would further the U.S. ability to advance national security objectives in Asia.

One country in Asia that serves as a significant variable is China. China is forecast to overtake South Korea as the second largest LNG importer by 2020, but it remains highly uncertain how much U.S. LNG would go to China. China's natural gas consumption is forecast to become about three times larger than that of Japan in 2020 and more than four times that of Japan in 2040.[5] But unlike Japan, which needs to import almost all of the natural gas it consumes, China has a notable volume of domestic gas output, which currently meets about two-thirds of its domestic consumption.[6] Also, home to the largest volume of technically recoverable shale gas resources in the world at 1,115 trillion cubic feet,[7] China now targets shale gas production levels of 2.12 tcf to 3.53 tcf (60 bcm to 100 bcm) per year by 2020.[8] The pace of shale gas development can significantly alter the current pattern of its gas consumption. Moreover, unlike

---

[4] "Japan's 2013 LNG imports hit record high-MOF," *Reuters*, January 27, 2014, http://uk.reuters.com/article/2014/01/27/energy-japan-mof-idUKT9N0GJ03120140127

[5] Institute for Energy Economics—Japan, *Asia/World Energy Outlook 2013*.

[6] U.S. Energy Information Administration, 2014. http://www.eia.gov/countries/analysisbriefs/China/china.pdf

[7] U.S. Energy Information Administration (EIA), "Technically Recoverable Shale Oil and Shale Gas Resources: An Assessment of 137 Shale Formations in 41 Countries Outside the United States," June 13, 2013, http://www.eia.gov/analysis/studies/worldshalegas/

[8] Government of the People's Republic of China, 2012. http://www.gov.cn/zwgk/2012-03/16/content_2093263.htm

Japan or South Korea, China is able to import natural gas via pipelines. China's import volume today is roughly split half-and-half between pipeline gas from Central Asia and Myanmar, and LNG from Asia and Middle Eastern producers like Australia, Qatar, Indonesia and Malaysia. The freshly inked pipeline gas agreement with Russia will further the share of pipeline gas imports by China. Additionally, while China's LNG demand is expected to continue growing, the notable absence of Chinese investment commitment to U.S. LNG projects to date renders it difficult to envision China becoming one of the largest importers of U.S. LNG anytime soon.

Question 2: In the immediate future, what portion of U.S. LNG will be supplied to Japan, in particular?)

As noted earlier, the total volume of U.S. LNG contracted by the Japanese through 2013—if materialized—would amount to roughly 20 percent (17 mmt/y or 828 bcf/y or 2.27 bcf/d) of the Japanese imports today.[9] This volume is equivalent to about one-quarter of the accumulative volume from the seven U.S. LNG export licenses to the countries without a Free Trade Agreement with the United States (9.27 bcf/d) that have been approved to date.

However, it is important to note that not all of the volume contracted by Japanese companies need to be sold to buyers in Japan. Several Japanese companies have reportedly been in talks with buyers from other countries about a potential purchase agreement.

Question 3: How can the United States best leverage its LNG resources to bolster U.S. influence in Asia?

The ascent of the United States as a major natural gas producer has already demonstrated U.S. strength to the regional players—albeit quietly.

For example, the robust production of shale gas has led to a 28 percent decline in the U.S. natural gas import level since 2005. This increasing self-sufficiency in natural gas consumption has freed up supplies that were once destined for the United States—particularly from Qatar, Western Africa and Trinidad—to reach other markets around the world, including Asian countries. Specifically, during the supply uncertainty after the Fukushima nuclear disaster, re-directed LNG supplies from the Persian Gulf prevented a serious supply shortage in Asia.

Also, many Asian stakeholders see supply security value in the U.S. shale gas revolution and U.S. LNG supplies. Asia's heavy reliance on the Middle East and Southeast Asia for natural gas makes their imports susceptible to supply disruption from conflicts in such geopolitically contentious areas like the Straits of Hormuz or the South China Sea. In contrast, U.S. LNG supplies—much of which would be loaded in tankers in the U.S. Gulf of Mexico—would presumably travel through the open sea after transiting through the Panama Canal, thus avoiding these global chokepoints. U.S. LNG supplies, therefore, strengthen their sense of energy security by diversifying both the sources of supplies and the associated transportation routes.

Additionally, the robust development of shale gas—together with tight oil—has dampened the "United States in decline" narrative that emerged after the economic recession of 2008,

---

[9] The Office of the Prime Minister, Japan, 2014. http://www.kantei.go.jp/jp/singi/keikyou/dai10/siryou.pdf

especially in China.[10] By delivering a range of macroeconomic benefits like GDP growth and job creation, the U.S.'s new energy posture has challenged the view held by many Chinese elites that the economic recession pointed to a waning U.S. global influence. The "declining U.S." narrative was further contradicted by the prospect of U.S. LNG exports to Asia.

Moreover, the ascent of the United States as a major energy supplier is starting to defuse the geopolitical undertone in East Asian gas importers' relationships with Russia. Russia's desire to enhance its Asian market share, coupled with growing Japanese demand, has suggested growing synergy between the two countries. Several gas export proposals are currently on the table for negotiation. Russia, whose LNG supply currently accounts for about ten percent of Japanese import, is the most—if not the only—viable candidate for supplying pipeline gas to Japan. Some in Japan see that the potential for stronger U.S.-Japanese energy ties would provide both security and leverage for the Japanese as they pursue negotiations with Russia despite a high degree of skepticism that Russia can deliver a fair deal. In fact, the U.S. LNG export potential could curtail temptations for those within Russia who may be inclined to use its energy resource wealth as a tool to advance its geopolitical objectives vis-à-vis Japan.

Meanwhile, there is an inherent danger in extrapolating that LNG resources accord significant geopolitical leverage to the United States. There is a limit to which privately held and market allocated resources, such as oil and gas, could be successfully employed by a democratic government to deliver a specific geopolitical or strategic outcome. In fact, energy-related geopolitical rhetoric can generate expectations that are unrealistic or too costly for the United States to fulfill.

The most significant and lasting way in which our LNG resources can bolster U.S. influence in Asia, therefore, is for the United States to demonstrate its commitment to upholding institutional norms and capacity that ensure the free flow of oil and gas. In other words, presented before the United States is an opportunity to distinguish itself from many traditional energy supplier countries and governments that are demonstratively inclined to wield energy supplies as a foreign policy weapon. The United States has long served as the torchbearer for free trade and the key founder of transparent energy market architecture. The stability that U.S. LNG supplies can induce and/or enhance in Asia is an understated yet significant asset that can underpin the continued U.S. leadership in the region.

Question 4: How will an increased supply of U.S. LNG affect the demand for Malaysian, Australian, and Qatari LNG supplies in the region?

The robust production of shale gas has led to the 34 percent increase in U.S. natural gas production between 2005 and 2014.[11] For example, the shale gas supplies from the Marcellus

---

[10] While many Chinese thinkers adhered to the view that U.S. power had waned, they were not the primary authors of the argument. Instead, they pointed to multiple assessments, to include those done by entities such as the U.S.'s own National Intelligence Council that the relative advantage in global power the U.S. had enjoyed was shrinking. DNI, "Global Trends 2025," November 2008.

[11] Calculations based on U.S. Energy Information Administration (EIA), *Annual Energy Outlook (AEO): 2014 Early Release*, 2014. http://www.eia.gov/forecasts/aeo/er/pdf/tbla14.pdf.

shale alone equal the entire natural gas export capacity of Qatar, which is the second largest natural gas exporter in the world.

The growing U.S. natural gas supply challenges the economics of many LNG export projects outside the United States. Developing an LNG terminal is a hugely capital-intensive undertaking, in the order of several billion dollars. The LNG projects currently being built outside the United States generally require infrastructure development from the start. In contrast, many of the proposed U.S. LNG export projects are designed to capitalize on LNG terminals designed or built in the last decade to prepare for LNG imports. The only major addition required to ready these U.S. LNG terminals for exporting natural gas is liquefaction capacity. Therefore, U.S. LNG export projects have economic advantage over new projects abroad.

For example, the Australians are acutely aware how the U.S. LNG supplies can compound economic challenges faced by many of their LNG projects under development. Australia currently has nearly $200 billion worth of LNG projects under construction and many of the projects have experienced some degree of cost overruns due to acute capital cost escalation stemming from a combination of factors like labor shortages, greater environmental hurdles, and the remote locations of some projects. Also, U.S. shale gas has likely contributed to Gazprom's decision to delay the Arctic Shtokman LNG project indefinitely.

However, caution is warranted in extrapolating the extent to which the U.S. LNG supplies may fundamentally alter the energy relationship between importer countries in Asia and their traditional gas suppliers. In fact, the scope of U.S. LNG influence on Asian demand for supplies from other countries is difficult to ascertain.

First, by the early part of next decade, the global LNG market and Asian LNG market are expected to see new volumes of supplies from new LNG projects in places like Australia and fierce competition may emerge among LNG suppliers. The pace of U.S. LNG export approval to the countries without a Free Trade Agreement with the United States, combined with the commercial viability of a specific project, greatly influences the degree to which U.S. LNG supplies can gain a foothold in Asia.

Second, cost advantage from Henry Hub based trade is far from assured on a long-term basis. As a series of export projects come to fruition later this decade, Henry Hub price levels will likely come under upward pressure to reflect the rising level of demand even if an adequate level of domestic supply continued.[12] Consequently, the gap between the Henry Hub price and delivered prices of LNG supplies from non-U.S. sources may narrow to the point where the price differential no longer offsets the costs of liquefaction and transportation from the United States.

Third, energy export is central to the economic health of many of the traditional supplier countries and many Asian stakeholders believe that the centrality of energy revenue combined with their vast resource levels continue to make them important trade partners. For example, the energy sector accounts for roughly 60 percent of the total government revenue for Qatar while

---

[12] As suggested by several studies on the economic impacts of LNG exports on the U.S. economy, including *Macroeconomic Impacts of LNG Exports from the United States* (Washington, DC: NERA Economic Consulting, December 2012), http://www.fossil.energy.gov/programs/gasregulation/reports/nera_lng_report.pdf.

energy export revenue accounts for over 70 percent of the total export revenue and half of the federal budget revenue for Russia.[13]

Finally, there are factors exogenous to the U.S. energy posture that are likely to greatly influence the level of LNG supplies from Qatar and Malaysia in the future. In case of Qatar, new projects are currently on hold in the North Field, where nearly all of Qatar's natural gas reserves are, while operators examine ways of sustaining high levels of production. Moreover, Qatar's North Field and Iran's South Pars constitute one of the largest natural gas deposits in the world. The pace at which Iran's natural gas production may ramp up pending the resolution of its conflict with the West would greatly influence the Qatari determination on the level of its production and export as over-supply could drive down the price of gas exports. As for Malaysia, economic development and modernization trends are driving domestic energy consumption growth. The country appears to be striving to maintain its natural gas production level through the development of new fields to meet the domestic demand as well as to fulfill its external obligations.

Closing

A range of factors renders it difficult to forecast the future composition of LNG suppliers to Asia. These factors include the pace of energy related infrastructure development and the scope of environmental regulations within the United States, as well as the impact of U.S. LNG supplies on the natural gas production profile of traditional gas supplier countries. Aside from these supply-side variables, moreover, the trajectory of future LNG demand outlook for individual countries in Asia is far from certain as it will be influenced by a mixture of factors, such as the role of nuclear energy in Japan, the pace of shale development in China and the potential of pipeline gas to Japan and South Korea, as well as the trajectory of the economic slowdown in China. Meanwhile, the U.S.'s new energy posture has already yielded both economic and energy security benefits for LNG importer countries in Asia. The United States has a further, important role to play for the greater security of energy supply in Asia and around the world by continuing to espouse principles such as free trade and transparency that are essential for the sound working of the international energy marketplace and the resultant free flow of oil and gas.

Thank you for your time and the opportunity to address the Subcommittee. I look forward to your questions.

---

[13] U.S. Energy Information Administration, 2014. http://www.eia.gov/countries/cab.cfm?fips=rs

Mr. CHABOT. Thank you very much.

Ms. Leopold, you are recognized for 5 minutes.

STATEMENT OF MS. DIANE LEOPOLD, PRESIDENT, DOMINION ENERGY, DOMINION

Ms. LEOPOLD. Thank you and good afternoon, Chairman Chabot, Ranking Member Bera and members of the subcommittee. Thank you for the opportunity to appear before the subcommittee.

I am here today because of Dominion Cove Point. This is an LNG import terminal that has been located on the Chesapeake Bay in Maryland for nearly 40 years. Thanks to the recent and growing abundance of natural gas supplies in the United States, LNG imports to the U.S. have nearly come to a halt.

Where Cove Point used to unload about 85 LNG tankers a year, we now can go months without one. The story is much the same at most other U.S. import terminals. Rather than a business disaster, however, we see a once in a generation opportunity. It is a significant opportunity for the United States to benefit economically, environmentally and geopolitically.

Dominion plans to invest nearly $4 billion in Cove Point to add export capabilities, primarily equipment to liquefy natural gas delivered by an existing pipeline. Ours is one of more than 40 proposed LNG export projects in the U.S.

For a variety of reasons, however, many experts believe that ours will be one of only about half a dozen to be built. Numerous studies have quantified the positive impacts that LNG exports will have on the U.S. economy. Even just a handful of LNG export terminals will create many thousands of construction jobs, hundreds of permanent jobs at the terminals.

There will also be thousands more jobs in the manufacturing of the equipment. Once operational, the terminals will support tens of thousands of additional jobs throughout the supply chain of producing, processing and transporting natural gas to the terminals.

Billions of dollars of new tax revenue will flow to Federal, state and local economies and the U.S. trade deficit will be reduced by tens of billions of dollars annually.

In searching for customers, we literally circled the world. Ultimately, we signed 20-year contracts with Sumitomo, a Japanese global trading company, and GAIL, one of the largest natural gas companies in India and majority owned by the government.

Sumitomo, in turn, contracted with Tokyo Gas and Kansai Electric to serve the needs of their respective customers within Japan. Japan needs natural gas for power generation to help make up for the closure of its entire nuclear fleet following the Fukushima disaster.

India, the fifth largest importer of LNG, needs it largely for power generation, often supplanting coal and to support the country's rapidly growing economy.

Given the global competition to support these markets, it is unlikely the U.S. will be able to supply the lion's share of LNG demand for India or Japan. Our facility will only produce a sliver of global demand. But that was fine with our business partners.

What both customers told us was that they wanted a stable, secure, reliable source of LNG as an important part of their portfolio.

This was not only because the U.S. offered a plentiful reliable source of natural gas itself but also because the natural gas was coming from a key political ally.

Both countries are focused on energy security and creating a diverse portfolio of supply sources. In addition, they wanted a market where they could buy natural gas at a price not linked to oil. That is why they turned to the United States and Dominion.

At the same time, the exports will not have a significant impact on U.S. prices. Export volumes will be relatively small in comparison to the nation's production capabilities and the cost of liquefying, transporting and regasifying natural gas is a total of about $7 per 1,000 cubic feet.

This will allow U.S. manufacturers to keep a significant price advantage. Natural gas that sells in the U.S. for $4.50 will have a delivered price of $11 to $12 in Asia.

Finally, I would be remiss in not noting that LNG exports will also have environmental benefits. U.S. natural gas displacing coal abroad in power production can reduce greenhouse gas emissions by as much as 50 percent. LNG shipped from Cove Point alone could reduce global greenhouse gas emissions by millions of tons each year.

In summary, we believe LNG exports to Asia and the Pacific will have a significant benefit for the United States and our trading partners.

It will help the U.S. economy and trade deficit, it will help reduce global greenhouse gas emissions and it will strengthen the energy security of our allies.

Thank you.

[The prepared statement of Ms. Leopold follows:]

TESTIMONY OF
DIANE LEOPOLD
PRESIDENT
DOMINION ENERGY

BEFORE THE
SUBCOMMITTEE ON ASIA AND THE PACIFIC
COMMITTEE ON FOREIGN AFFAIRS
U.S. HOUSE OF REPRESENTATIVES

REGARDING THE EXPORT OF LIQUIFIED NATURAL GAS

MAY 29, 2014

Good afternoon Chairman Chabot, Ranking Member Faleomavaega, and members of the Subcommittee. My name is Diane Leopold and I serve as President of Dominion Energy, the business unit of Dominion Resources that houses our natural gas operations, including the Cove Point liquefied natural gas terminal on the Chesapeake Bay in Calvert County, Maryland.

Dominion is a "Fortune 250" company headquartered in Richmond, Virginia. It is one of the nation's largest producers and transporters of energy, with a portfolio of approximately 23,600 megawatts of nuclear, gas, coal, wind, solar, biomass, hydro, and fuel cell power generation; 10,900 miles of natural gas transmission, gathering and storage pipelines; and 6,400 miles of electric transmission lines. Dominion operates one of the nation's largest natural gas storage systems with 947 billion cubic feet of storage capacity; and serves nearly four million electric and gas utility customers in Virginia, North Carolina, Ohio, and West Virginia.

Thank you for this opportunity to appear before the Subcommittee today to discuss an important and positive set of developments for our nation.

Overview

Dominion is proud to be at the forefront of the remarkable turnaround in our nation's energy fortunes. As recently as 2005, the U.S. Energy Information Administration (EIA) was projecting that by today the United States would be importing as much as 10 billion cubic feet per day (Bcf/d) of natural gas in the form of liquefied natural gas (LNG). By 2025, the EIA projection for LNG imports was approaching 18 Bcf/d, or more than 20 percent of the nation's natural gas needs. Instead, thanks to remarkable technological advances developed in the U.S., the nation now finds itself with an abundant supply – enough to meet domestic needs for at least the next century while being able to export a limited amount to important allied nations around the world. The nation's conversion from net importer to net exporter of natural gas is expected to occur by 2016. This is because of the initiation of LNG exports as well as reduced imports from Canada and increased exports to Mexico via pipeline.

This relatively quick turnaround in our nation's natural gas supply picture brings with it major domestic and international implications.

From an economic standpoint, numerous studies have reached similar conclusions in terms of the positive impacts this new activity will have. More than 40 LNG export facilities have been proposed in the United States, although most experts expect the number built and put into service will be not more than a half-dozen – including Dominion's Cove Point facility. Initially, the construction of even a handful of LNG export facilities will create thousands of jobs, not just in the building of the terminals but also in the manufacturing of equipment that will be installed in the plants. For example, our project will install large liquefiers manufactured by the Air Products Company in Pennsylvania and two General Electric Frame 7 power turbines built in South Carolina.

Once operational, the terminals will support tens of thousands of additional jobs throughout the supply chain of producing, processing, and transporting gas to the terminals. Billions of dollars in new tax revenue will flow to federal, state, and local economies. And, the U.S. trade deficit will be reduced by tens of billions of dollars annually.

The potential for geopolitical benefit for the United States and our allies is just as significant. Our nation's strategic position in the world will be strengthened as we shift from being dependent upon others for a growing share of our energy to becoming a major supplier to others. The relationship between energy trade and international affairs was illustrated vividly by a front-page photograph in *The Wall Street Journal* earlier this month showing Russian President Vladimir Putin and Chinese President Xi Jinping toasting a 30-year agreement for Russia to sell $400 billion worth of natural gas to China starting in 2018. As *The Washington Post* reported about the ceremony, "China's president also called for an Asian security arrangement that would include Russia and Iran and exclude the United States." The United States has the opportunity to counter that kind of alliance by being a source of clean, reliable natural gas for our allies who are urgently in need of such supplies. For us to stand aside would leave our allies no choice but to turn to those who would meet their needs.

I make no pretense about being a foreign affairs expert. However, Dominion's ongoing experience with our export project at the Cove Point facility can provide a real-world example of the kind of opportunity LNG exports can provide to the United States. Please allow me to focus on that Dominion project.

Dominion Cove Point

The Cove Point facility was constructed by a predecessor of Dominion and a partner in the early 1970s as an LNG import terminal. After about two years of receiving shipments of LNG from overseas, imports came to a virtual halt because of changing economic conditions. The Dominion predecessor sold its interest and the plant was essentially mothballed from that time until 1994, when the onshore facilities were reactivated to provide limited storage services for local gas utilities. In 2002, Dominion acquired all of the Cove Point facility and began work to reactivate it as an import terminal as the nation began to look overseas to help meet its growing energy needs. The reactivated terminal received its first LNG shipment in the summer of 2003. At its peak in 2005, Cove Point received about 85 shipments, mostly from Trinidad and Tobago. Based on the projected future demand at that time, Cove Point import capability was then almost doubled in size.

Then everything changed again. Domestic gas production began to climb due to tremendous advances in technology. Prices began to fall. It became clear that LNG imports would likely not be needed in the foreseeable future. Dominion, along with owners of several other LNG import terminals, began to explore the feasibility of adding export capability. In 2011, we began marketing the Dominion Cove Point export project to potential overseas customers. We literally circled the world in looking for customers. We held discussions with numerous parties from across Asia and Europe, ultimately completing agreements with two customers in 2013.

Dominion Cove Point Customer Overview

Sumitomo, a Japanese global trading company and GAIL, one of the largest natural gas companies in India and majority-owned by the government, each signed up for one-half of Cove Point's export output for a period of 20 years. Specifically, each company will have the right to receive a minimum of 2.3 million metric tonnes of LNG annually during that time.

Sumitomo in turn signed offtake agreements with Tokyo Gas and Kansai Electric, the ultimate users of the gas. As you may be aware, Japan's entire fleet of 48 nuclear reactors remains shut down as a result of the Fukushima disaster in 2011. Much of the shortfall in electricity is being made up by generating additional electricity from imported LNG and an increased use of coal. In fact, Japan is also constructing a number of new coal-fired power plants and is today the world's second-largest importer of coal. Although the Japanese government recently announced plans to restart at least some of its idled nuclear reactors, the country is expected to remain the No. 1 importer of LNG globally.

In the case of India, currently the fifth-largest importer of LNG, the additional supply is needed to fuel the country's economic growth. Estimates are that India's natural gas needs will triple by 2022. Currently, almost 70 percent of India's power generation comes from coal, according the International Energy Agency. It is expected that additional gas-fired generation will offset coal.

Our facility will be able to produce only about 5¼ million tons of LNG a year, which may sound like a lot but is only a sliver of global demand. But that was fine with our business partners. What they told us was they each wanted a stable, secure, reliable source of LNG to help round out their portfolio, not dominate it. They also wanted a market where they could buy gas at a price not linked to oil. That is why they turned to United States and Dominion. This is a very important point. They both see the United States as a good ally and a good trading partner. In fact, GAIL recently announced it expects to sign additional supply contracts this year for more LNG exports from the United States.

The contracts signed with Sumitomo and GAIL are tolling agreements, meaning Dominion will only provide liquefaction service to our customers. We will not sell them gas. Rather, the customers will be responsible for procuring the gas and transporting it to the terminal through the existing pipeline. In fact, both customers have made investments in upstream sources to bolster their security of supply across the value chain. Dominion will liquefy the gas and load it onto the customers' ships for transport to its ultimate destination.

U.S. and Global Competition

Likewise, other energy companies have been marketing U.S. export capacity to consumers around the world. Asia is certainly the frontrunner in the competition to secure contracts with projects for LNG exports from the U.S. To date, 43 applications totaling nearly 40 Bcf/d have been filed with the DOE for a license to export LNG. However, it is likely that only a fraction of those will actually be built. Of the projects that have announced off-take contracts, four expect to deliver LNG to Asia, for about 60 percent of the contracted volumes. A further capacity breakdown of this subset of projects shows that of that 60 percent, Japan will receive 37 percent, India will receive 11 percent, and Korea will receive 11 percent.

Worldwide competition is fierce to supply natural gas to these countries, both using LNG and in the case of India, via pipeline. As I said, our customers have focused on pricing, security and diversity of supply in their buying decisions. Any one of these factors alone will not attract long-term contracts. And pricing includes the mechanism by which a price is reached. Japan, for example, has repeatedly expressed its desire to eventually break the oil-linked pricing that most of its imports are now based on. Exports from the U.S. will generally be tied to lower Henry Hub prices. However, even with construction of the expected handful of U.S. terminals, U.S. exports to Asia will still remain a small portion of those countries' overall supply portfolio.

History has certainly shown how strong the political and economic ties can be when associated with energy supply – some good and some not so good. The countries listed above are strategic allies for U.S. foreign policy. Our ability to provide reliable, long-term supply of energy will only help to strengthen our relationship with these key allies and help insulate them from other energy suppliers who may use their influence in conflict of the best interest of the United States.

Little Price Impact in the United States

There has been a good deal of discussion recently about the impact that LNG exports will have on natural gas prices for American consumers. Some critics have said the export of LNG will lead to customers in the U.S. paying a much higher "world price" for natural gas. That is not a realistic outcome and here is why. As I mentioned, our customers will buy the gas themselves and transport it to Cove Point. The current price per million Btu of gas, or 1 MMBtu, is roughly $4.50. First you need to add to that the cost of liquefaction, or roughly $3 per MMBtu. Then add another $3 or so per MMBtu to ship the gas to Asia and another approximately $1 to regasifiy it at its destination. By the time that $4.50 gas arrives in Japan, for example, the delivered cost is in the range of at least $11 or $12 per MMBtu.

The pricing dynamic I just described is entirely different than crude oil, for example, which can be shipped around the world for a small fraction of the price of the actual commodity. In the case of crude there is more of a world price. It is the significant expense of liquefying, transporting, and regasifying natural gas that will serve to prevent the development of a so-called "world price."

Furthermore, this $6-$7 liquefaction and transport cost exists regardless of the price of natural gas sold in the U.S. If the natural gas price increases domestically, there will be plenty of worldwide competition happy to deliver to these markets.

Some have suggested that exporting LNG would amount to giving up America's competitive energy advantage in manufacturing. Nothing could be further from the truth. For the reasons I just explained, today a U.S. consumer of gas would be paying roughly $4.50 per MMBtu while its overseas competitor would be paying as much as three times that amount for the same gas. If a company can't be competitive with that type of advantage perhaps there is some deeper issue with that company's business model.

Permitting

American consumers also are protected by the dozens of federal, state and local permits needed prior to constructing an LNG export terminal. The two main federal permits come from the U.S.

Department of Energy (DOE) and the Federal Energy Regulatory Commission (FERC).
Numerous other agencies participate in the process.

Under the Natural Gas Act, permission to export LNG is granted by the DOE. In order to export
to a country with which the U.S. does not have a free trade agreement, DOE must determine that
such exports are, on a project by project basis, in the public interest. In the case of Cove Point,
we filed for this permit in October of 2011. Just under two years later, in September of 2013, we
received conditional approval from DOE.

The other main federal permit needed is from FERC. The Commission has the responsibility of
reviewing each project for purposes of environmental impact and safety. In June 2012 we began
the pre-filing process at FERC, and filed our formal application in April 2013. As part of
FERC's very thorough process we submitted more than 20,000 pages of information on all
aspects of the project. On May 15 of this year, FERC staff released its Environmental
Assessment (EA) for the project, concluding that approval of the project "would not constitute a
major federal action significantly affecting the quality of the human environment." We are now
in the middle of a 30-day comment period on the EA. It is our hope that soon after the close of
the comment period the FERC will grant permission to begin construction.

Once we receive permission to proceed to construction we will begin work on what will be a
$3.4 billion to $3.8 billion investment. Construction will take approximately three years and
will, at peak, employ a union workforce of about 1,250 workers. We expect to be ready to
produce LNG by late 2017. Once operational, Cove Point's annual property tax payment to
Calvert County will increase by roughly $40 million, making Cove Point the largest taxpayer in
the county.

Environmental Benefits

I would be remiss if I did not mention one other benefit of LNG exports from the United States.
This displacement of coal-fired generation overseas with imported LNG is worth emphasizing.
Earlier this year Dominion commissioned ICF International, a highly respected energy and
environmental consulting firm, to review the lifecycle Green House Gas (GHG) emissions from
LNG. ICF concluded the following: "Based on the best available data and using standard
assumptions, exported LNG would have GHG emissions 43 percent to 52 percent lower than
coal." In the case of Dominion Cove Point, LNG exports used to displace coal for electricity
production could reduce GHG emissions by millions of tons a year.

If the goal is reduce GHG emissions, LNG is one of the ways to get there. In fact, President
Obama's own climate action plan released in 2013 stated that "we will promote fuel-switching

from coal to gas for electricity production and encourage the development of a global market for gas."

Summary

LNG exports from the United States clearly have important and positive implications for the nation economically, environmentally and geopolitically. Good trading partners make good allies and good allies make good trading partners.

We are proud of the fact that Dominion Cove Point is an early mover in expanding U.S. exports. Dominion's ability to export LNG represents a major opportunity for Maryland and positions Dominion as a major contributor in the effort by the United States to become a net exporter of energy. Thanks to technological advances, the U.S. has enough natural gas to meet not only America's consumer demand, but also to export some supply in the form of LNG without significant impacts on domestic prices.

It is clear that natural gas is a cleaner, more economical fuel than coal. This means, LNG exports can provide significant global environmental benefits, such as cleaner air. By exporting LNG, the U.S. will be providing the world with increased access to a source of cleaner and reliable energy, without compromising Americans' ability to utilize this important resource here at home.

LNG exports are consistent with the President's National Export Initiative to expand exports to create "sustainable economic growth" as well as "good high paying jobs". LNG exports also support America's important and vital role as an energy superpower and can support our allies by providing a competitive, reliable and stable energy supply.

Dominion welcomes the release of the federal environmental assessment – an assessment that found the facility can be built and operated safely with no significant environmental impact - the company is poised for an exciting future.

Thank you.

Dominion Cove Point LNG Terminal, Lusby, Maryland

Mr. CHABOT. Thank you very much, and I will yield to myself for 5 minutes to begin with the questioning. I would ask any of the folks who would like to comment to do so, relatively briefly, if you would.

What U.S. policies or regulations, currently in effect, are limiting our ability either presently or in the future to do what we are talking about here today, which is trying to export more LNG from the U.S., create jobs here and improve our trade to Asia? I open that up to anybody that would like to take it.

Mr. HERBERG. Well, I don't think there is too much magic in this. I think it is—you know, we need to encourage the gas production side. I mean, think about this.

The Marcellus gas field is—within a year or two will become the largest natural gas-producing field in the world, larger than North Dome Qatar field, the west Siberian oil and gas fields.

So we have this enormous capacity to increase gas production. So I think policies that will encourage effective regulation, which provides public confidence that shale gas drilling can be done environmentally—in an environmentally sound way, that is a critical part of this to increase shale gas production.

And, obviously, the permitting process, the environmental process, Department of Energy, FERC—this whole process is really a very long process that could be speeded up, I believe, and the market opportunity is there. It is an intense competitive environment. So I think those are the kinds of things that would make this happen faster.

Mr. CHABOT. Okay. Thank you.

How has the Japanese evolving energy policy since Fukushima impacted their ability, interest, or their need to get more natural gas from us, and where are they now? Because immediately there was this almost knee jerk reaction we are going to shut them all down and that, apparently, has evolved to maybe we will shut some down, not others. Who would like to take that? Ms. Nakano.

Ms. NAKANO. Thank you for the question.

Prior to the Fukushima, Japan did have a fairly diversified energy profile where nuclear supplied about a third of its power generation and then fossil fuel had probably about 50 percent. They were looking at renewables combined, including hydro power as well.

Nuclear was definitely central to their energy security strategy. But Fukushima very much changed the environment—both political environment but then also technically the 54 nuclear reactors had to come offline. And so the idea to promote the use of nuclear in its domestic power mix had to be reconsidered.

Prior to—again, prior to Fukushima the idea was to increase its share of nuclear to about 50 percent of its power generation. So following Fukushima, the Japanese turned to cheaper sources of natural gas but particularly the U.S. They do have a long-standing business relationship with countries such as Qatar, Australia and also Russia supplies about 10 percent of their import needs.

But the United States looked particularly attractive to the Japanese because of the gas-to-gas competition—deregulated gas prices within the United States. Looking forward, their energy policy making is very much in flux and the national leadership hopes to come—bring some share of nuclear reactors back online.

However, the public sentiment or the public anxiety over the safety of existing nuclear reactors still runs quite high. There are a couple court challenges that are in the way of companies and also their nuclear regulatory body to restart nuclear reactors.

Mr. CHABOT. Thank you. Let me cut you off there, if I can. I have a little less than 1 minute left and I wanted to get one more question in.

Trade agreements like the Trans-Pacific Partnership, or TPP, cover a wide range of issues. My question is, what is the potential impact of TPP on U.S. LNG exports and trade in the Asia-Pacific region?

Ms. Leopold, do you want to take that since—you could have answered the other ones.

Ms. LEOPOLD. I could have answered the other one as well as these—or this one.

Mr. CHABOT. All right. Well, who would like to take this one? Mr. Herberg.

Mr. HERBERG. Well, in terms of the Japanese market, all these approvals of non-FTA export arrangements in a sense makes the TPP moot in the sense of LNG exports, I believe. There is not any really specific elements of that.

Assuming—you know, so Japan, South Korea is a free trade agreement partner so there is no issue there. These approvals have covered many other places like India and elsewhere that are non-free trade agreement countries.

So I think from the Japanese perspective particularly, they see the TPP as something that is enshrines—in a sense enshrines the durability of U.S. commitments to export LNG because there is a little bit of worry that we might—if U.S. gas prices really spike in the future, that there be a domestic debate about cutting back on those LNG exports even though they have been approved. There is some concern of that on the Japanese part.

Mr. CHABOT. Thank you. And I will conclude that arguably, if TPP ultimately does get approved on all sides and it does increase the trade opportunities, the economies will hopefully thrive and grow, and therefore there will naturally be more of a need for energy to feed that growing economy. As a result, hopefully we will be able to export more gas to the region.

I will cut myself off there and now recognize the gentleman from California, Ranking Member Mr. Bera, for 5 minutes.

Mr. BERA. Thank you, Chairman Chabot.

Mr. Herberg, you just touched on, I think, the complexity of balancing our domestic needs and domestic advantages that this LNG and energy revolution that is happening here in the United States offers us but balancing that with, obviously, some market opportunities abroad.

Let me make sure I got the pricing correct here. Our domestic price currently is about $4.50. The current Asian market price is about $15.

Is that—so, you know, when I had a chance to visit India this past summer and chat with some of the Indian multinationals and as they are making their strategic manufacturing decisions and so forth, a component in that is as some of the Asian advantage in lower payroll starts to wane and payroll goes up—goods that they are manufacturing to sell to us here domestically they really are factoring in the lower energy costs.

And as they are building those factories and so forth there is a real opportunity for us to be very competitive, to—you know, when you factor in cost of transport from, let us say, India or China to the United States, costs of higher energy costs, we need to make sure we don't shoot ourselves in the foot here when we have this policy.

And I think—I would be curious on your thoughts on that and I do know there is a benefit here as well because there are market opportunities overseas. So Mr. Herberg.

Mr. HERBERG. I mean, this is, obviously, an important part of the discussion and I think it is important to be balanced. But it is also important, I think, to understand the market dynamics of this because, yes, you have $15, $16 LNG prices today in Asia.

But in effect that is an aberration. That started in 2009 and accelerated to 2011 with the Fukushima. Remember Japanese LNG demand went from 70 million tons to 90 million tons in 2 years. That was a shock on the demand side in the Asian LNG market.

Now, if you look forward to 2015, 2020, 2022, you are going to have a lot of LNG coming to Asia from Australia, Russia, the U.S., elsewhere. I think there is a prevailing view in the industry that LNG prices are likely to come back down toward a more normal range of, say, $13—$12, $13.

Now, U.S. gas prices—up to about $6 you got $6 or $6.50 liquefaction and transportation. At about $12 or $13 LNG prices in Asia and $6 gas in the U.S. the investment decision to send gas—LNG to Asia becomes a wash. So in effect it is partly self-limiting and, you know, $6 gas here is not as good as $4.50 gas.

But I think it is still wildly cheap on a global competitive basis. And so I think the market dynamics are important to understand here.

Mr. BERA. I just want to make sure that this is a major component, you know, particularly where in my home state of California we are still grappling with 8 percent unemployment and you are still—you know, we have seen decades of loss of manufacturing jobs and there really is an opportunity for us to revive on a manufacturing basis here in the United States.

Certainly, again, we don't want to lose the market opportunities overseas as well and there is—certainly, with our allies we certainly want to help support them. But at the same time, we don't want to sacrifice this competitive advantage. Ms. Leopold, did you want to add?

Ms. LEOPOLD. Yes. The two things that I would add is, as Mr. Herberg had discussed—Marcellus and the fact that it is growing—the supply is there.

There is a very large surplus and technology is continuing to improve to increase the economic recoverable reserves here. So there is ample gas right now to meet these market needs. And I will echo that the international market is somewhat self-limiting.

There is a lot of international competition to meet these LNG supplies such as Australia and others that at a certain natural gas price the competitive advantage of having the $4.50 gas goes away. If natural gas prices go up too much they will look elsewhere.

Mr. BERA. So let us stick with this line of—you know, let us say prices in Asia normalize and come down to the $12 or $13. So if I am sitting at my natural gas company here domestically there is going to be overwhelming pressure to say, you know, I can sell here domestically at $6 or to Asian markets at $13.

We do have to be very conscious that, you know, that is going to be a very compelling drive, that we don't want to sacrifice this real potential to revive the manufacturing base here in America. So I will just inject that into the conversation. Thank you.

Mr. HERBERG. Could I just make one quick comment? I have told my friends in Japan very often Henry Hub U.S. flexible pricing is no guarantee of low LNG prices because, you know, there is the U.S. market issue.

But even with that, in a sense we will be wildly competitive even in that scenario. You can't go below $12 or $13 in Asia because you can't get it—nobody can really deliver it in there for less than that, given that huge transportation issue, and Europe is stuck at $9 or $10.

So we are still going to have a huge competitive advantage in, I think, in what you can call a worst case.

Mr. CHABOT. Gentleman's time has expired. The gentleman from Pennsylvania, Mr. Perry, is recognized for 5 minutes.

Mr. PERRY. Thank you, Mr. Chairman. I will start out with Mr. Herberg and your comments regarding Marcellus shale. Being from Pennsylvania, I will note not from shale country but still very interested.

One of the—we have a governor's race going on and one of the candidates has—that is running for governor has proposed an extraction tax now. Pennsylvania currently does not have an extraction tax. They have got an impact fee associated with the drilling and the production, pipelines, et cetera.

The extraction tax potentially—I guess potentially, depending on the size of it or the amount of it would—but would it make—you talked about the Marcellus shale field being the largest, potentially, in the world or it will the largest in the world.

It is not going to change the fact that the size is there but is it going to be—is that extraction tax going to be a deterrent to development in Pennsylvania?

Mr. HERBERG. You know, I don't know, you know, the scale that they are talking about for that so I don't want to get myself in trouble. Any incremental, you know, load on the total capital costs and operating costs of a project is going to affect somewhat the drilling. I think it all depends on the scale of that.

I would just say one important issue is to deal with the local impacts of shale gas drilling. This is a very intensive industrial process. It has huge community impacts on roads and water supplies, and I think in some places there is real imbalance between where some benefits of the revenues from that are going and whether that is getting to these areas that are being directly affected by the operation, which are significant.

So I think it is important for the governments to find ways to make sure these local areas are getting, you know, a share of the revenues to take care of some of the increased costs for all kinds of things that come out of this process.

Mr. PERRY. Okay. Ms. Leopold—did I say that right? Okay. Leopold. Sorry about that. Would you say that U.S. prices are artificially low? Just curious.

Ms. LEOPOLD. No, I would not say they are artificially low. I would say the market is working. There is plentiful supply and our natural gas prices are lower than elsewhere because we can economically drill lower.

Mr. PERRY. Okay. So there has been—based on that, there has been some supposition even among members of the panel here that exporting more or exporting to a greater degree natural gas, LNG, CNG, is going to absolutely without question increase our prices here.

Is there—what is the validity to that claim and are there any facts and figures? Because I didn't hear any here on that side of the argument but you might have some counter.

Ms. LEOPOLD. The one thing I can say is that rigs have continued to pull back because natural gas prices are low and it is not enough for the producers to be profitable. So with natural gas prices coming up, more drilling can occur, which increases the supply.

Mr. PERRY. And increased supply equals what?

Ms. LEOPOLD. Well, there is not enough demand.

Mr. PERRY. I mean, if you used the principle of supply and demand, right?

Ms. LEOPOLD. Right.

Mr. PERRY. I mean, so it should equal——

Ms. LEOPOLD. Lower prices.

Mr. PERRY. Thank you. Okay. So you got that. All right.

Are there any main concerns with the DOE's process for export approval to non-FTA countries and can you provide any examples of when an approval was denied based on public interest? Anybody on the panel.

Mr. HERBERG. I don't know of any, no.

Mr. PERRY. Okay. How about otherwise? Other than public interest?

Mr. HERBERG. I don't believe any have been denied. A couple of them they have approved a lesser volume than was applied for.

Mr. PERRY. And what is the point of that? Can you—if you know. What is the point of doing that? Why would they—why would they approve a lesser volume?

Ms. LEOPOLD. Cove Point had a lesser volume because it matched the volume that we applied for in our Federal Energy Regulatory Commission application. So the DOE just went to sync with what we requested in that application after our design work was complete.

Mr. PERRY. So it could do more but it has just not because that was the application and at that point is that—that is not necessarily the government's fault if there is a fault? That is what you applied for?

Ms. LEOPOLD. Correct.

Mr. PERRY. Okay. In India, with infrastructure investments needed in order to effectively receive and distribute large volumes of LNG or what infrastructure—do you know what—because that is an emerging market? Do you have an indication? It is a large emerging market.

Mr. HERBERG. They suffer from a lack of natural gas pipeline capacity and infrastructure, port LNG terminal capacity and, most importantly, they maintain energy prices.

They administer and control energy prices and hold them so low for natural gas that more expensive LNG coming into the market can't find a home and that really limits the ability to really raise natural gas consumption in India. They need to—they need to deal with price reform domestically to get the price——

Mr. PERRY. They need to let the market dictate the——

Mr. HERBERG. They need to let the market work a little more. It is a wildly administered system.

Mr. PERRY. Thank you, Mr. Chairman. I yield.

Mr. CHABOT. Thank you. The gentleman's time has expired. The gentleman from California, Mr. Sherman, is recognized for 5 minutes.

Mr. SHERMAN. EPA just announced some regulations that the chamber says are going to shut down all the coal electric plants in the United States.

That may be a bit overdrawn but do the analyses that our witnesses provide reflect that regulation assume that it is going to be implemented and that there is going to be a substantial increase in U.S. demand for non-coal generated electricity?

Mr. HERBERG. I can't say. It is something I work on very much but I——

Mr. SHERMAN. So we could see a situation—you have told us that the price in the United States is $4.50. That could go to $6.50 just as a result of today's regulations and that the natural—use for natural gas is to generate electricity and it is competition with coal. So if that were true we could cancel the hearings. But let us go on.

Now, Mr. Herberg, you basically have given us some prices in Asia, prices in the United States. I interpret from that that you are saying it costs about $6.50 a unit to liquefy it, ship it and deliquefy it or return it to a gaseous state.

Is that pretty much the same whether you are shipping to Asia or you are shipping to Europe? Europe is a little shorter distance. Is the real cost in the liquefaction and the gasification or is the real cost—or is there a substantial cost per mile?

Mr. HERBERG. The largest share would be liquefaction. Maybe Dominion would talk about that more.

Ms. LEOPOLD. Very roughly, in the total of $7 range, $3 would be the liquefaction, $3 would be the shipping to Asia and $1 would be the regasification.

Mr. SHERMAN. Okay. So the—so it would be a little cheaper to send. One public policy position we could take is to give licenses if you want to ship to Ukraine or to European pipelines that could then reverse flow to Ukraine but not to Asia.

I am not sure that that is the right public policy. Are any of you aware of any economic—I mean, the studies from the U.S. Department of Energy say if we allow unfettered export we are going to see a one-third increase in natural gas prices.

Are any of you aware of any economic studies as to what effect that has on the competitiveness of our manufacturing and fertilizer plants? How many jobs do we lose when we start paying $6, $7 a unit rather than $4.50 a unit for natural gas? Anybody aware of any studies on that?

Mr. HERBERG. No, I haven't seen any but——

Mr. SHERMAN. I think we would also see, of course, a slight reduction in the cost of LNG in Asia, which would make our competitors just a little bit more competitive. I think the effect there would be a little less.

The background memo that our staff provided for this hearing describes the United States as currently an importer of natural gas and that we will shift to a net exporter only by 2020.

Is that accurate and who is—which foreign countries are willing to sell us LNG—are willing to sell us natural gas at a price so low that we can keep prices at $4.50?

Mr. HERBERG. Canada.

Mr. SHERMAN. Canada.

Mr. HERBERG. Yes, and——

Mr. SHERMAN. And so what we could see is the Canadians will get tired of selling us natural gas at $4.50 and decide to build their own liquefication and send it and it wouldn't matter.

Is there substantial discussion of liquefication or liquefaction in Canada and would that also be a reason to cancel the hearings on the theory that if all the Canadian natural gas goes to Asia there is no economic reason to send U.S. natural gas?

Mr. HERBERG. Well, the—yes, there are a number of LNG projects proposed on the British Columbia coast and even in the east for LNG from Canada. But I think, again, this is kind of a self-limiting process.

At $3, Canadian gas backed up into Canada was net backing to the point where investment collapsed in natural gas development in China—I mean, in Alberta for a while but at $4.50 the incentives start working back. But they are seeing their market basically absorbed by this huge expansion in U.S. production.

So yes, they have to look elsewhere for long-term future markets. But, again, if the U.S. price rises then that is going to pull Canadian gas in and this is a huge system they have built. So it is partly market self-limiting.

Mr. SHERMAN. I am—I think I would support export if I knew that that would get us more jobs in the energy industry than it would cost us in those industries that use the comparatively cheap natural gas that is being used in manufacturing and fertilizer production.

And, Mr. Chairman, in spite of all those comments about cancelling the hearing I am very glad you are having this hearing and I yield back.

Mr. CHABOT. Thank you. I am glad we have your approval. The gentleman from California now is recognized for 5 minutes, Mr. Rohrabacher.

Mr. ROHRABACHER. How much natural gas is used to produce fertilizer? Do you know? We don't. My gosh. It is a substantial amount of natural gas is used to produce fertilizer? But we do know a substantial amount of fertilizer is used to produce natural gas.

I mean, you can't have fertilizer without natural gas, right? Or can you? Unless you got a lot of horses and cows around. Then it is another kind of gas.

Mr. HERBERG. The bulk uses power generation. Industrial petrochemicals feedstocks is where most gas goes—industrial use, boilers. So it is not a huge portion that would be fertilizer but I—you know, I couldn't give you a——

Mr. ROHRABACHER. How much of natural gas then goes to just energy, like electricity production?

Mr. HERBERG. That would be the bulk of it. I mean, that would be the largest share and even industrial processes you are doing heat—you know, using gas for heat generation, plant operations, things like that. That is energy indirectly so a large share of it. I don't have the numbers in front of me.

Mr. ROHRABACHER. Yes, I would sure like to know some of those statistics. Also, natural gas—someone told me that you now can turn natural gas into diesel fuel?

Mr. HERBERG. Mm-hmm. Yes.

Mr. ROHRABACHER. What is the cost of that?

Mr. HERBERG. Very high, relatively. They are doing that kind of thing in Qatar because they have an enormous surplus of natural gas—gas to liquids, you call it.

Mr. ROHRABACHER. Right.

Mr. HERBERG. Shell has a project. Malaysia has a project. But it is a pretty expensive thing. It produces very clean diesel and gasoline but at a very, very high cost relative to today's kind of prices.

Mr. ROHRABACHER. There is—I was just notified a few weeks ago about a business that was going to try to capture the burning—the flare-off gas in North Dakota and would then use it to produce diesel gas. Do you think that maybe that would be economically viable?

Mr. HERBERG. In small—in small kind of niche areas. You have a huge bunch of gas being produced in North Dakota that there is no pipeline capacity—take-away capacity for it so it gets flared.

So if it is zero value gas essentially because it is going to be flared, you can make sense out of that economically to produce diesel or products——

Mr. ROHRABACHER. Okay.

Mr. HERBERG [continuing]. Even though at a normal kind of process where you are paying market price for natural gas it wouldn't make sense.

Mr. ROHRABACHER. Okay. How much natural gas is Australia producing?

Mr. HERBERG. They are exporting about 25 million tons a year of LNG from the Northwest Shelf—mainly Northwest Shelf project.

Mr. ROHRABACHER. Exactly how much are they producing? We don't know how much actually they are producing.

Mr. HERBERG. It is a small gas market, in effect, for Australia. You know, it is just a bunch of cities around this——

Mr. ROHRABACHER. Right. But I understand that there has been new oil and gas finds in Australia that are massive. Is that correct?

Mr. HERBERG. Yes. There is seven large gas projects being—LNG projects being built as we speak in Australia—seven—for well over

50 million tons of LNG that will come on stream from 2015 to 2022 or so—huge.

Mr. ROHRABACHER. So we are talking about huge new things in the United States but also our friends there to the south and Australia will become a major new force on the market in making all these calculations.

Mr. HERBERG. Absolutely.

Mr. ROHRABACHER. And I also understand that in Australia that they have discovered some kind of—a great water source underneath the ocean. Is that correct?

So anyway, I just—I was reading some scientific journals where apparently there has been—underneath their ocean they have found a freshwater ocean. That would be—but you don't know anything about that?

Mr. HERBERG. No.

Mr. ROHRABACHER. Well, let me just say that fertilizer, and we have all of these products and as I said in my opening remarks we are talking about the amount of wealth that exists in the world and we should applaud the increase in wealth and applaud anything that would facilitate the distribution of wealth in a more efficient way because this is what will hopefully uplift the human condition.

So thank you very much for your information today to put into our little equations that we make here. Thank you.

Mr. CHABOT. Thank you very much.

The gentleman from Georgia, Mr. Collins, is recognized for 5 minutes.

Mr. COLLINS. Thank you, Mr. Chairman. I just have a few questions and just open up for the panel anybody that would like. Surveys suggest that the growth in LNG demand is mainly concentrated in China and South Korea.

There is some other—along with some other southeast Asian markets. Which countries are the greatest, largest potential recipients of U.S. LNG exports and which countries offer the greatest mutual benefit for U.S. strategic interest in this area?

Ms. NAKANO. In my judgment, Japan will be the largest buyer of U.S. LNG supplies. Japan already does have a large import receiving capacity. But then also, unlike China, Japan does not have the option of importing gas—natural gas by pipelines.

And also the current investment commitment into the U.S. LNG both upstream but then also export projects suggest that they will take about a quarter of the amount—the cumulative amount from the seven projects that have been approved to date to non-FTA countries.

Mr. COLLINS. So Japan—from your position Japan stands with its capacity and also its infrastructure that is already in place would be the natural beneficiary in this?

Ms. NAKANO. Yes, and China certainly has a potential to become a large or one of the leading global LNG importers but that doesn't mean that they will be necessarily turning to the United States.

Mr. COLLINS. Well, given the interesting political discussions over the sea and other issues there I think this provides an interesting conversation.

I do have another question there that sort of is similar. How does Australia's strong energy export market with China affect its strategic relationship with the United States and does Australia see any contradiction between a strong relationship with China and its strong strategic relationship with the United States? Or is it all about the business?

Mr. HERBERG. They would like—the Australians and the Chinese would like to keep it all about business. But in the real world, as Australia's economy both in energy and minerals becomes more closely linked to Chinese economic prosperity and markets, there is a discussion in Australia about the balancing of the U.S. alliance with its growing dependence on China and this, obviously, looms in the overall kind of contest in Asia for influence between China and Russia.

So there is a discussion about that in Australia. But fundamentally Australia remains deeply committed to the U.S. alliance for now.

Mr. COLLINS. Well, in light of that let us chase that a little bit further. If there is a much more—a much heavier influence of U.S. LNG into this market which would maybe also, for lack of a better term, undercut or change that dynamic with Australia and China, do you think that attitude could change in Australia or would there be a tightening or a shifting of the geopolitical atmosphere there that could move that a little bit?

Mr. HERBERG. No, I think that is a good point. For our purposes and I think for Australia's, it is important that all the big suppliers like Australia and others have a very diversified slate of buyers for their output and that is the sensible commercial thing to do—have a broad set of buyers from a whole bunch of different countries and regions.

So I think on the part of Australia they want to keep a diversified slate. But to the extent we create a more diversified slate by—with our exports into the region, I think that is good for all of us in terms of keeping those alliances in shape.

Mr. COLLINS. Well, I think the alliance is in shape. I was also concerned, and I think it was brought up and I am not going to go into it here, pricing and issues with domestic pricing as opposed to what would be found on the international market, especially with the price disparities that are out there.

A curious question—you brought this up and it just—it triggered a thought from me. In looking at the Australia, Japanese, the Chinese market here in this balance, with Russia giving and China importing more in from Russia, traditionally not the closest of allies or friends even in that region, how—given what we have seen on the more eastern side with Ukraine, Crimea and the dependence aspect that is over there, could this be a balance from the U.S. perspective in dealing with China in this—in this market, a balance to Russia becoming a dominant player in the Chinese energy market? Is that—how does that affect the political aspect?

Mr. HERBERG. Yes. I think at the margin it does. The more U.S. LNG in the region, and China doesn't have to be necessarily a direct buyer of U.S. LNG. If we are going to Japan then that frees up LNG that China will be buying from Australia.

Offshore East Africa will come on after 2020 region. You got Papua New Guinea. You have got lots of areas of supplies. So I think our supplies in there create a more diversified mix and that is a good thing.

The closer Chinese-Russian gas relationship—the gas pipeline deal that was just signed—by the time that stuff comes on that will still only represent 10 percent of China's natural gas consumption.

So I think the Chinese are very careful about diversifying their supply sources. They are very deliberate about this and the last thing they want to do is put themselves vulnerable to Russian pressure.

Mr. COLLINS. Well, I am out of time. But, Mr. Chairman, I would appreciate this conversation because it not only just takes this with the LNG issue.

This raises what I believe is something that we don't discuss enough and that is the changing geopolitical influences of a region that is, one, the largest growing region, the most populous region, and potentially the most unstable of the regions in the world whether it be economic, political, religious, other things going on here.

So I think it has just brought up an interesting point. Mr. Chairman, I do appreciate it and I yield back.

Mr. CHABOT. Thank you. The gentleman yields back.

We will go into a second round. I just have a question or two but I probably won't use the whole 5 minutes. Then if Mr. Sherman is interested, he can do that as well.

I also wanted to reiterate something that Mr. Sherman mentioned and that is about our colleague, Randy Weber. When we were in Asia some months ago, he brought up at every meeting we had, whether it was Prime Minister Abe, President Park, President Ma, to everybody from downtown, or to the taxi drivers, at the places about LNG gas—the importance of it—specifically, Texas LNG gas. So he was really doing great work out there trying to export something we have here and trying to create jobs here. So my hat is off to him for that.

I just had one quick question here and anybody is welcome to take this. Maritime and territorial disputes in the region, mostly between China and Japan, China and Vietnam, China and the Philippines, and China and Taiwan, et cetera—what impact, if any, could there potentially be on exploration and development of potential natural gas resources or energy resources in general in the region? How much of those disputes have to do with that issue versus fishing rights, and things of that nature, and actual acquisition of land? What part of it is energy related? Ms. Nakano, would you like to take it? Thank you.

Ms. NAKANO. Thank you. In my view, energy is not the driver. Many surveys have indicated that there is somewhat limited amount of proven oil and gas reserves in East China Sea or South China Sea.

However, because of these geological—I am sorry, geopolitical tensions there has not been really satisfactory amount of surveys done. So it is a bit of a—sort of a, you know, horse and cart issue.

But I think that the prominence or the importance of places such as the South China Sea is really that it is—it is where the—about half of global LNG transits.

So it will remain to be important. But as far as for the production of resources that may or may not be there, that is something that I do not think is the main reason why there is a tension among the countries in that region.

Mr. CHABOT. Let me interpret that if I can, or correct me if I am wrong. You are saying, that in your view, it is not the driving principal, but since tensions have prevented a lot of the exploration from taking place, they really don't know how much is there and it might potentially be a big deal but we don't really know that at this time, but there may be other things that are driving instability more than that issue right now. Is that correct?

Ms. NAKANO. Yes, correct. And if I may add quickly, that from my understanding there are some technical challenges to exploring the oil and gas resources there or doing a survey because I understand there is submarine valleys and also very strong currents.

So there are also sort of technical and sort of geological challenges associated with further surveys there.

Mr. CHABOT. Okay. Thank you. I will yield back my time. If the gentleman from California has any questions you are recognized.

Mr. SHERMAN. Okay. South Korea has the KORUS agreement and so you don't have the same approval process that we would to export natural gas to Japan. Is natural gas cheaper or is it expected to be cheaper over the next several years in South Korea than in Japan?

Mr. HERBERG. The Japanese prices are much higher than—domestic gas prices are higher in Japan because they pass through the cost of these high costs of LNG. In Korea, they tend to administer prices for gas and oil and coal and electricity——

Mr. SHERMAN. Administer through government subsidy?

Mr. HERBERG. Yes. Well, through government price direction and guidance because remember, you only have——

Mr. SHERMAN. Well, you can have price correction and guidance but if you are a utility in South Korea and the price of LNG is high in part because of Fukushima you can't pay less on the theory that your government wants you to pay less.

Mr. HERBERG. In a very simplistic way, KOGAS, the state gas company, contracts for the LNG and imports it at world prices or Asian prices.

Mr. SHERMAN. Right.

Mr. HERBERG. It sells that gas to KEPCO, the state electricity underwriter. KEPCO is required to keep electricity prices relatively low for——

Mr. SHERMAN. Okay. So I shouldn't buy any stock in KEPCO.

Mr. HERBERG. KEPCO gets—KEPCO catches it on that because they are required.

Mr. SHERMAN. Okay. In any case, looking only at the wholesale price or the importer's price because you can jack up electricity prices, subsidize them, whatever, do those who import that LNG to South Korea pay any less on average than those who import natural gas to Japan?

Mr. HERBERG. No, no. The price——

Mr. SHERMAN. And so the—it is not like the South Koreans say great, we have got KORUS, Japan doesn't—they will have to pay Qatar and Malaysia a lot and we can be the sole Asian importer of U.S. natural gas. That isn't happening. The South Koreans are paying as much and signing long-term contracts to pay as much as the Japanese? Ms. Nakano.

Ms. NAKANO. Thank you. South Korea already has investment into Sabine Pass and that is the one that is already scheduled to start exporting as early as next year.

Mr. SHERMAN. They have investment in what again?

Ms. NAKANO. Cheniere's Sabine Pass project. That was who—which got approval back in 2011. So and from what I understand that contract does include some linkage to Henry Hub price. So down the road they——

Mr. SHERMAN. But it is not that, okay, you have got the U.S. Government screwing up the free market. We limit or prohibit U.S. exports to Japan. We allow U.S. exports to South Korea. Therefore, there is a huge differential or a huge benefit to South Korea.

As far as we know, they are paying and expect to be paying pretty much per unit the same as the Japanese are paying and the effect of the U.S. limitation on exports to Japan doesn't seem to be playing a main effect.

Let us go on to another line of questions and that is I have dreamt that we—somehow we and the world off of its addiction to petroleum as a transportation fuel and there is one production automobile that is powered by compressed natural gas and its cost per mile, I am told, is half.

I don't know if you are familiar with that statistic and can reflect on it but to what extent would preventing the export of natural gas keep prices in this country low enough so that we will see the development and implementation of natural gas-powered vehicles?

Mr. HERBERG. You know, it is a complicated relationship between limiting exports of LNG and the domestic prices.

Mr. SHERMAN. Right. And you don't know whether your main effect is to limit production or to limit price.

Mr. HERBERG. Yes. You can—you can bottle up the—you know, the natural gas and get somewhat lower prices but you will also reduce investment in new supplies, and how that balance works out is not always very clear.

Mr. SHERMAN. Is there a lot of natural gas to be developed in the United States that gets developed at $7 domestic price but doesn't get developed at $4 domestic price?

Mr. HERBERG. Yes, yes. There is a huge transfer of our gas supply.

Mr. SHERMAN. Is that half of our potential? A quarter of our potential? Does any of the other witnesses have a comment?

Mr. HERBERG. I have seen studies of that. I could try to get those.

Mr. SHERMAN. Yes. Please provide that for the record because——

Mr. HERBERG. They have a cost curve and my recollection is that something of 70 percent of the known resources or reserves out there are producible at $7——

Mr. SHERMAN. The one question I will ask you to ask—answer is what will be the effect on total U.S. production if we eliminate our restrictions on exports.

I believe you have already estimated the price change would be from around $4.50 to $6.50 but if you can refine that, and I am going to ask the other witnesses to also provide answers to the—to record to that to the extent you can be helpful, and I am going to yield back.

Mr. CHABOT. And all the witnesses are nodding their affirmative response. We thank the gentleman. The gentleman's time has expired.

I want to thank all the witnesses here this afternoon for testifying. Members will have 5 days to supplement their statements or submit questions, and if there is no further business to come before the committee we are adjourned.

Thank you.

[Whereupon, at 3:42 p.m., the committee was adjourned.]

APPENDIX

MATERIAL SUBMITTED FOR THE RECORD

SUBCOMMITTEE HEARING NOTICE
COMMITTEE ON FOREIGN AFFAIRS
U.S. HOUSE OF REPRESENTATIVES
WASHINGTON, DC 20515-6128

Subcommittee on Asia and the Pacific
Steve Chabot (R-OH), Chairman

May 22, 2014

TO: MEMBERS OF THE COMMITTEE ON FOREIGN AFFAIRS

You are respectfully requested to attend an OPEN hearing of the Committee on Foreign Affairs, to be held by the Subcommittee on Asia and the Pacific in Room 2172 of the Rayburn House Office Building (and available live on the Committee website at www.foreignaffairs.house.gov):

DATE: Thursday, May 29, 2014

TIME: 2:00 p.m.

SUBJECT: Energy Needs in Asia: The U.S. Liquefied Natural Gas Option

WITNESSES: Mr. Mikkal E. Herberg
                  Research Director
                  Energy Security Program
                  The National Bureau of Asian Research

                  Ms. Jane Nakano
                  Fellow
                  Energy and National Security Program
                  Center for Strategic and International Studies

                  Ms. Diane Leopold
                  President
                  Dominion Energy
                  Dominion

By Direction of the Chairman

The Committee on Foreign Affairs seeks to make its facilities accessible to persons with disabilities. If you are in need of special accommodations, please call 202/225-5021 at least four business days in advance of the event, whenever practicable. Questions with regard to special accommodations in general (including availability of Committee materials in alternative formats and assistive listening devices) may be directed to the Committee.

49

COMMITTEE ON FOREIGN AFFAIRS

MINUTES OF SUBCOMMITTEE ON _____ *Asia & the Pacific* _____ HEARING

Day__*Thursday*__Date____*5/29/2014*____Room____*2172*____

Starting Time ___*2:00 p.m.*___ Ending Time ___*4:00 p.m.*___

Recesses |____| (____to ____) (____to ____) (____to ____) (____to ____) (____to ____) (____to ____)

Presiding Member(s)
Chairman Steve Chabot (R-OH)

Check all of the following that apply:

Open Session ☑   Electronically Recorded (taped) ☑
Executive (closed) Session ☐   Stenographic Record ☑
Televised ☑

TITLE OF HEARING:
Energy Needs in Asia: The U.S. Liuqefied Natural Gas Option

SUBCOMMITTEE MEMBERS PRESENT:
Rep. Ami Bera (D-CA), Rep. Scott Perry (R-PA), Rep. Brad Sherman (D-CA), Rep. Dana Rohrabacher (R-CA), Rep. George Holding (R-NC), Rep. Doug Collins (R-GA)

NON-SUBCOMMITTEE MEMBERS PRESENT: *(Mark with an * if they are not members of full committee.)*

HEARING WITNESSES: Same as meeting notice attached? Yes ☑ No ☐
(If "no", please list below and include title, agency, department, or organization.)

STATEMENTS FOR THE RECORD: *(List any statements submitted for the record.)*

TIME SCHEDULED TO RECONVENE _____
or
TIME ADJOURNED ___*4:00 p.m.*___

_____
Subcommittee Staff Director

Statement for the Record
Submitted by Mr. Connolly of Virginia

Both the domestic and world markets for natural gas have fundamentally changed in the previous decade. U.S. Natural Gas Marketed Production grew from 19,517,491 million cubic feet in 2003 to 25,616,403 million cubic feet in 2013, constituting a more than 30 percent increase in domestic production. The United States is projected to become a net exporter of natural gas by 2020, and our allies in the Asia-Pacific have increased their demand for natural gas in recent years.

For example, higher demand in India has been spurred by economic growth and the need for energy sources with emissions that are cleaner than the burning of coal, currently India's largest energy source. In Japan, the meltdown at the Fukushima Daiichi nuclear power plant in 2011 led to the subsequent shuttering of the nation's 48 nuclear power facilities and a 33 percent increase in liquefied natural gas (LNG) imports from 2011 to 2012.

Given the paradigm shift in how we view natural gas production and trade, it is incumbent upon this Congress and the United States Government to conduct a comprehensive evaluation of the growth of the natural gas industry and develop policies that promote environmental safety, transparency and energy security.

In September 2012, I joined with several of my colleagues to write to the Secretary of Energy requesting the Department of Energy's Office of Fossil Energy (DOE/FE) prepare an Environmental Impact Statement (EIS) to determine how LNG exports may potentially increase environmental risks in communities where natural gas is extracted. As we look beyond our borders and consider the benefits to trade that LNG exports may offer, we must first consider the impact at home. A comprehensive EIS is one way to do that.

An additional option is to support common sense legislation that addresses the environmental and health impacts of increased natural gas production. I am a cosponsor of H.R.1921, the Fracturing Responsibility and Awareness of Chemicals (FRAC) Act of 2013 which requires the public disclosure of chemicals used in hydraulic fracturing operations. The FRAC Act also ensures that healthcare professionals will have access to proprietary chemical formulas when obtaining the information is necessary to treat a medical emergency. The FRAC Act has bipartisan support and I commend it to my colleagues for their support.

The United States is currently the largest producer of natural gas in the world. Natural gas production has increased and prices have remained low at a time when U.S. dependency on foreign oil is at a 20-year low. This has certainly afforded the U.S. some latitude on issues of national energy security. As our friends and allies in the Asia-Pacific pursue similar ends and seek to attain energy security through American sources of natural gas, we must consider their alternatives. Strengthened energy ties with the region's bad actors are not in the best interests of U.S. national security and the security of our allies. This is by no means a near-term solution to issues such as Russian aggression, as the timeline for most export projects extends into the latter half of this decade. However, it is a point that merits attention.

As we consider LNG exports, it is my hope that Americans maintain access to safe and affordable energy sources. The industry should be a partner in this endeavor and help us weigh the benefits of increased trade with the potential health costs of increased production. I look forward to hearing from our witnesses today on how we can plot a path forward that includes transparent practices and careful consideration of environmental and public health impacts of new and existing projects.